Twin Flames

A TRUE STORY OF SOUL REUNION

ANTERA

BALBOA.
PRESS
A DIVISION OF HAY HOUSE

Balboa Press books may be ordered through booksellers or by contacting:

Balboa Press
A Division of Hay House
1663 Liberty Drive
Bloomington, IN 47403
www.balboapress.com
1 (877) 407-4847

ISBN: 978-1-5043-4371-8 (sc)
ISBN: 978-1-5043-4444-9 (hc)
ISBN: 978-1-5043-4443-2 (e)

Library of Congress Control Number: 2015918814

Print information available on the last page.

Balboa Press rev. date: 12/15/2015

To my beloved twin flame, Omaran, and to all other twin flame and soulmate unions on the planet.

Acknowledgements

First and foremost, I give thanks to Spirit and my spirit guides, who love me no matter what, and who are the best support system anyone could hope for.

Second, my deepest gratitude to Omaran, my twin flame, husband, and partner, for living the drama with me and being willing to share the story in hopes that others will learn from it. He gave his total support to the effort, and offered many comments and suggestions.

And many thanks to the following people, who also helped in the creation of this book:

Michael Wopat edited the manuscript, and contributed some content ideas. He lived his part of the drama with an open heart, and continues to teach many by his example.

Phil Dizick patiently worked with me on the cover design, and helped with graphical and technical problems.

Byron Belitsos read the manuscript and gave feedback on content, as well as publishing advice.

Janet Stark edited the manuscript for content, improving it greatly and helping me put things in perspective. She provided encouragement and support in many ways.

Linda Stark supported me spiritually and energetically throughout the process.

Loretta Stark proofread the typeset book and found important errors. As my mother, she is a positive force in my life, and taught me I could do anything I wanted if I followed my heart.

Ralph Stark, my father, gave me the strength to carry on despite the obstacles and taught me to be an independent thinker, qualities that help me in every project I attempt.

In the second edition, Juliette Looye reviewed and greatly improved the preface.

Song Credits

All lyrics quoted in the text are from songs composed and recorded by Antera and Omaran. Most are from the companion album, *Twin Flames*, the sound track of their two-person musical, which beautifully captures this story in music.

Preface to the Second Edition

Since I published this book twelve years ago, there has been a vast increase in the awareness of the twin flame connection. The subject evokes in many people a deep yearning for their perfect mate, their beloved, and a fulfilling relationship at all levels, from the physical to the spiritual. This yearning comes from memories deep in the soul.

Also during this time period, there has been a considerable amount of misinformation written about twin flames. However, even with the proliferation of false ideas and generalizations, I have found that just the notion of having a twin flame is often enough to push people onto a spiritual path, which is beneficial. The concept of twin flames has been the way into a soul perspective.

I've received thousands of emails from people who met someone who shook up their world, caused them to reassess their priorities, and whetted their appetite for spiritual or psychic subjects. They all wanted to know if this person was their twin. Most often the purpose of these meetings is to give a spiritual push, and not necessarily to bring the two people together for long. These were often soulmates and extremely important people in their lives, but not twins.

What many people haven't understood is that until one is nearing ascension and enlightenment, there is no way the twin will appear physically. It would be impossible to be together for long, and it would not serve the highest purpose. The connection between twin souls is primarily spiritual, which makes it intense beyond words. This is why reunion only happens when both have undergone many lifetimes of healing and cleansing, and the spiritual connections are strong in both.

The twin is not the "other half." This is not someone who will complete us. The path of the human being involves gathering experience, making mistakes, then moving back to wholeness within ourselves. Only when we have a balance between the male and female within, and we have healed most of the trauma and mistakes from all our lifetimes, should we even consider that we may meet our twin flame.

But even though it is extremely rare for twins to come together, soulmates are coming together at unprecedented rates. This is indicative of the emergence of a new paradigm in couples as the consciousness of humanity evolves. Those who make their spirituality a high priority are no longer fulfilled by the old kind of relationship that only had connections at one or two lower levels: physical, emotional or mental. Being with someone who shares the soul path—and is willing to put this at a top priority—is the only option for many on the planet now.

In this book, I share the story of me and Omaran, my twin flame, during the beginning of our journey together, which started in 1993. It is not sugar-coated or idealized. Instead, it includes painful situations and the mistakes we both made as we uncovered all that was not love. This is what the intensity of the twin flame relationship does. If anything is not love, it is not tolerable, so everything that has not been healed comes up for healing fast after a twin flame couple reunites.

Our story gives a taste of this Divine Union, but also helps dispel the myth about living happily ever after. The idea that if we could only find the perfect match, the right person, we would love each other unconditionally for the rest of our lives, is still firmly ingrained in many cultures. Most romantic movies and books end with the two people getting married, as if that were the end of the story. This is a misleading fairy tale.

Omaran and I made it through the intense healing process, and we have now been together for more than twenty years, living, loving, and doing our spiritual service as authors, psychic healers, teachers, initiators, and planetary healers. Spiritual service is the primary reason twin flames reunite, so they can do their parts to bring higher consciousness to the planet and humanity in a much larger way than individuals are able.

Also embedded in this story is our close association with the Ascended Masters, and many of their words of wisdom are included. They are the inspirational beings who have gone through the human journey, graduated and ascended to a higher dimension, and now they act as way-showers for humanity. I have had the ability since childhood to communicate with them, and they have been my teachers in this lifetime. These masters brought Omaran to me, helped us overcome obstacles, and have guided our spiritual service over these last two decades. For their guiding Light, I am eternally grateful.

My hope for this new edition is that it will continue to spark the soul memories of humanity and feed the flame of Spirit. At the time of the first edition, few people were interested in the spiritual path. Now we are finally seeing the mass awakening that many of us lightworkers have anticipated for decades. The concept of twin flames is an integral part of this awakening. May this story deeply inspire all who read it, not only with the possibility of deeper romantic love but with the desire to become Divine Love.

Antera
Mt Shasta, California
2015

One

We barely met and yet
I know him intimately.
We hardly spoke and yet
I hear him constantly.
His face keeps appearing
right in front of me.
How can I work
with all this telepathy?

— From the song
"Who Is That Man?"

Who is that man??
Cathy had been feeling a bit out of control all week, which was very unusual for her. Her concentration at work, usually impeccable, was fuzzy, as that man kept coming into her thoughts. His handsome face, framed by that wild gray hair, and with those kind eyes that expressed laughter so easily, was almost becoming ingrained in her consciousness.

Now, as she sat in front of the computer preparing input files for a computer program that predicted ground motions from future earthquakes, she noticed a new sensation. It was an energy concentration of some kind at her navel, a buzzing that she could not quite ignore. Making sure none of her coworkers were around to see, she closed her eyes for a moment to see if she could get a better sense of what was happening there. With her inner sight she saw it—an energy cord coming out of her navel. It was made of golden Light, beautiful and intensely activated. Curious, she followed it out as far as she could perceive, and she found, with a start, that it was attached to HIM! To his navel! Was this new, or had it always been there, and she hadn't noticed it before? What did it mean?

She made another big effort to bring her attention back to the computer screen, and to continue her calculations. Luckily, this particular phase of the project didn't require intense concentration, because she had done similar earthquake analyses many times before. She hoped no one would notice her drop in productivity over the last few days—she rationalized to herself that her efficiency was usually very high, so a little distraction should not be noticed.

It was fortunate that she had the office mostly to herself, with only occasional interruptions from the others. It was solitary work, and she liked working as a seismologist in the small consulting company in Berkeley, across the bay from San Francisco.

She glanced out the window at the trees in the yard, which she could barely see from her desk. Consciously drawing their energy to her as she often did while working, she gave them her thanks as she felt their balm of life-force soothe her. The office was very functional and organized, which it had to be, cramped as it was into such a small space, but it was devoid of plants or colorful pictures on the walls, which would have enhanced the working environment for her. The walls were lined with shelves of books and scientific journals, leaving no room for frills.

The trees helped temporarily, but did not hold her attention for long. Besides the fact that her mental concentration wasn't up to her own high standards, she thought, it was distressing that anyone could have this kind of an effect on her. Especially someone she hardly knew. *Who is that man??*

It had all started with that hug. Last year she had attended a series of weekend workshops on building the Light body, after an intense seven-month course on tape called "Awakening Your Light Body," created by Sanaya Roman and Dwane Packer. The course had been one of the most important steps she had taken on her spiritual path, and the seminars were also very transformative. Toward the end of the last one,

HE had ended up sitting next to her, so they paired off for some of the meditation exercises.

They had casually hugged afterward—at least she had intended it to be casual—and she had immediately noted that she had never felt so at home with anyone before, including her husband. In the next instant, the resonance had started between them that jumped both their energy levels up several notches, taking her by surprise.

And THEN he had said, "I love you" with such meaning, as if it were coming from somewhere deep within him. And her own response had also surprised her: "We've been together before." What was she doing talking to someone she had just met that way? She still felt somewhat embarrassed by it, and now her cheeks flushed just from thinking about it. Quickly looking around the office to make sure no one was around to see this involuntary reaction to her thoughts, she shook her head and tried to focus on her work.

But that effort at controlling her mental wanderings didn't last for long. She found herself musing about how she had later reasoned that he probably said that kind of thing to all the people he meditates with, sort-of a casual "love ya" instead of Love with a capital "L." She had given him her phone number, because he suggested that maybe they could meditate together, but only after she had made it clear that there would have to be a group of others present. She needed to be proper about this, and not infringe on her loyalty to her husband.

She had thought about this man a lot for a couple of weeks after the seminar, but when months went by without a call, the memory had faded. She had thought it all a silly event blown out of proportion.

When he did finally call five months later, she had instantly recognized his voice. They had talked for an hour, the time going by very quickly as if they were old friends, finding out that they had many interests in common. It turned out he was a singer and songwriter, like herself, and they found that their paths up to now had been similar in many ways, too much so to be by chance, she thought. Their spiritual interests were uncannily alike.

After that call, they had met at a meditation group just last weekend, a group she had happened to be invited to for the first time—another coincidence. There they had barely talked at all, though she had felt his presence strongly throughout the meditation, so why was there this incredible pull to him? It was not something her rational, scientific mind could comprehend.

I am married, I am happily married, so what is happening here? She thought about her marriage of seven years, even as her fingers continued to work on the keyboard. At first, the personality differences and living styles between herself and her husband Mike had caused a bit of strife; he, so detail-oriented that he wanted to organize everything, and her, so oblivious to messes or organization around the house. But the differences had been settled, each changing habits to move more toward middle ground, and they had learned to live together in peace and love.

Then there was the larger issue she had been challenged with in living with him—he was what she called an "energy broadcaster," one who was very good at sending energy all over the vicinity but who often didn't know he was doing it. She was highly empathic and sensitive to energy, and, especially as a child, always seemed to have difficulty separating her energy from that of others around her. When Mike came home from work, the whole house was filled with whatever he was currently feeling, and if he was upset, she and her two sensitive sons would get upset, too.

Over the years, she had learned to differentiate her energy more effectively, so she could tell the difference between what he was feeling and what she was feeling, and now his energy broadcasts no longer affected her, unless she was unusually tired or in PMS. In fact, just a few months ago she had decided that she had finally mastered the art of maintaining her centeredness and emotional stability amidst the most unsettling of emotional dumping, not only from Mike but from others. She had worked hard at it, considering it a personal challenge, first learning how to shield her energy and avoid the disturbance from others, and then later finding that she could simply become transparent to the energy and nothing stuck; the energy just went right by and through without any effect on her.

This was a big lesson for her, and she was thankful to her husband for helping her learn it. Now they really enjoyed living together, and she accepted him and loved him just the way he was. She hoped that someday he would learn to use his energy more responsibly, sending it to useful, healing purposes, because she really felt he had a gift when it came to energy transmission. But she was finally at peace with him the way he was now.

There was only one thing about the marriage that kept nagging in the back of her mind. One thought occasionally crept out, wanting attention. She really wanted to have a mate with whom she could share her spiritual experiences—someone on the same or a similar path to hers, who could appreciate and add to her spiritual growth. Her rich life in the "inner planes" and other dimensions, so much a part of her, was just as real and important to her as "normal" consciousness.

Mike was open to hearing her stories of new things she had learned or great experiences she had in meditation, but though he tried his best to listen, he would invariably start yawning, and tune out a bit. She knew this was just from a lack of understanding because he had not experienced anything similar, even though he meditated regularly. Maybe, she thought, it was simply this need of hers for a more spiritual mate that was making her feel so swayed by this new man.

I'm very loyal to my husband. She said it several times to herself, trying to chase away any more thoughts of the other man and the mysterious Golden Cord connecting her to him. She continued trying to concentrate on her work, using all her mental powers. This had to be conquered. She had to stay in control. *Enough of these thoughts!*

She blinked, bringing the computer screen more into focus and checking her work displayed there. The accuracy of the seismic calculations was very important, and the allowable margin for error was almost zero. A miscalculation of a very small amount in any of the parameters that had to be estimated to predict ground motions could mean millions of dollars in retrofitting cost, or worse—significant damage to structures in a large earthquake.

But one more thought successfully caught her attention before she could let it all go. A part of her wanted to go to the group meditation and potluck dinner this weekend, but did she dare? She tried to convince herself that she was going for the meditation, but she also knew that the man on the other end of the Golden Cord would be there. Michael was his name, same as her husband Mike's, except that Mike preferred the shorter, less formal version.

There was a certain excitement that fluttered her stomach when she thought about going, an irrational quickening that only the heart could explain, even as her mind tried to squelch it. Maybe if Mike wanted to come with her, it would be all right. Yes, she'd ask him. And if he didn't want to go—well, maybe it was fate.

Two

Long ago and far away,
I held you, I thought forever.
A kiss, you said, could transcend time.
We both laughed, don't you remember?

— From the song "Long Ago"

"Please, please, please be there," Michael chanted aloud as he drove to the potluck dinner, drumming on the steering wheel to reinforce his intent.

He had been willing it all week, hoping Cathy would telepathically get the message. When he had seen her at the group meditation last weekend, he had known without a doubt that he needed to get to know her. There was a strong attraction like he had never felt, as if some unseen force was pulling him to her, almost against his will, and certainly against his better judgment. He was well aware of the ring on her finger. They had exchanged few words, but the energy between them was so strong, he had had difficulty concentrating during the meditation. In fact, he had opened his eyes once to peek at her, and she had looked very blissful. He had managed to ask if she would meet him for coffee sometime, but she had turned him down, saying she was married and didn't do that kind of thing.

He knew that the only reason he was attending this dinner today was to see her. The people were nice, and there would be a group meditation, but that alone was not enough to draw him there. It was quite a drive, after all, over Mt. Tamalpais to Stinson Beach. He realized that her drive would be much longer, across the bay. Surely it would be worth it to her. Surely she could sense what he was sensing.

As he drove his Toyota truck on the familiar, windy road over Mt. Tamalpais through the forest, he could smell wet redwood, fir, and madrone trees. A light rain was falling, a common occurrence in early February in Marin County, and he normally enjoyed the musty smells. But now his mind was preoccupied. He had never been affected by anyone in this way before, and it was disturbing that she was married. Well, maybe he could just develop a friendship with her, there was no harm in that. It may be a good spiritual connection, and maybe that would be fulfilling enough.

But the word "soulmate" echoed in his mind over and over whenever he thought of Cathy, though he didn't dare latch onto it. Nurturing that kind of hope was too painful after wanting a soulmate for so long, and being disappointed over and over. He thought about all his efforts to call for his soulmate. After finally ending, a few years ago, a lengthy, strife-filled marriage that had been held together by a futile hope and for the kids, he had become determined to find a woman who shared his spiritual path—one who had a philosophy of life and priorities compatible with his.

His spiritual growth had blossomed since leaving the marriage, and he attended as many spiritual seminars and workshops as he could find. Almost every woman he saw at these events was a possible candidate, and he found himself wondering whether she was The One. Somehow he knew deep inside that she was coming to him, and he thought that all his problems would then be solved. He and she would love each other so much that nothing else mattered. She would accept him just the way he is, and they would live happily ever after.

That thought made him smile, and he grinned at the trees as he passed them on the road. His arms and the truck seemed to know this road so well that they worked as a unit, smoothly flowing around the winding curves like water in a creek flowing around rocks on its way downstream. He didn't need to think about it, after driving this road countless times in his seventeen years of living in Marin County, both for his construction business and for the many hikes he loved to take on the mountain. It was a magical and healing place to him, and he never tired of the woods and the expansive views of the Pacific Ocean that inspired him so.

It was to one of his special places on the mountain that he had gone on a memorable day last year, to sort out his thoughts. He called the place "God Talking Rock," for the big boulder he liked to sit on there. It was easy for him to talk out loud to God and his spirit guides there, sorting through his problems, and he always received guidance and came away with renewed perspective and direction. The place had an energy field about it that seemed to make this communication much easier and more real.

He recalled standing on the rock, gazing out at the ocean, and being filled with a powerful energy. Frustrated about not finding his soulmate, about still being alone with this deep spiritual yearning, though he had been praying about it for so long, he had suddenly reached a point of ultimatum. With a powerful intention from his soul, he spread his arms, raised his voice and proclaimed to the universe, "IF I CAN'T HAVE MY SOULMATE, I'LL LIVE ALONE FOR THE REST OF MY LIFE!"

Since that day he had accepted that he may, indeed, be alone for his remaining years on the planet, and he hadn't looked for his other half so intently. Giving up the active search was also easier when, shortly after his proclamation on the mountain, he asked a friend for a channeled reading. One of his questions was whether his soulmate was coming to him and he was told that he was his own soulmate, and that becoming complete within himself, balanced between his male and female sides, was his most important task. He knew this was good advice, so he had focused more of his efforts into further self-growth, and was at peace with it—until Cathy had come along.

He thought about the way he had met Cathy at the seminar. He had noticed her immediately, with her long red hair and spirited green eyes. She was standing in line, and caught his eye. He held her in his gaze for a long moment. Although she was attractive, there was something else about her that kept his attention. Since then, he had mulled it over and over in his mind, and still that "something else" was intangible, indefinable. When he saw the ring on her finger, he had felt a surge of disappointment and looked away. They had a brief conversation later, during a break in the seminar, and he had enjoyed talking with her about their spiritual paths.

It was months later, at another seminar, when they had connected again. They had hugged at the end, and the words, "I love you," had flowed out of his mouth before he could stop them. Goosebumps had covered his skin and he was shocked, not only by saying such a thing, but at how deeply he had felt it. Her energy seemed to reach deep into the very essence of his core being as if they had always been together, and it was a simple statement of Truth. He had hoped she wouldn't be as shocked as he was, and to cover his embarrassment, he played it cool afterward. When she gave him her phone number, he hadn't really known what to think. And what was it she had said? *That they had been together before!*

Though he had thought about her intensely after the seminar, and wanted to call, he had held back because she was married. Plus, he didn't think he had completely finished healing his pain from previous relationships. He had almost convinced himself that their connection was all in his imagination.

But three months later, just last November, as he was walking along the sidewalk to his apartment, he had a "knowing" that said, "My soulmate is coming now!" It was very strong, almost urgent, and deeply affected him. He knew from experience that these intuitive hits were always important. Still, within a couple of days he had dismissed it, because he had truly accepted that he may not meet her in this lifetime, and couldn't allow himself to get his hopes up.

His spiritual guidance had been determined, however. He could see that now. Just two weeks after that knowing, as he walked along the exact same stretch of walkway, came The Voice. He heard a distinct booming voice say, "Call Cathy!" He had looked around instinctively, but there was no one there; The Voice was clearly a command from his Higher Guidance and coming from inside his head. "Call Cathy!" It had gotten his attention. Never before had he heard a voice like that, so he wasn't about to ignore it. Still, another two weeks had passed before he finally called, just after the new year. . . .

He was closing in on the destination, so he paid attention to the slip of paper that had the written directions on it. The house was easy to find. He parked and went in. It was a beautiful, yet slightly funky, house on the hill overlooking Stinson Beach, full of light and sea breezes, and brightened by many indoor plants. The living room had been set up for the group, with chairs and cushions arranged in a circle for the meditation. He had brought his favorite leek and potato soup and heated it up on the stove in the small kitchen.

The company was stimulating, and he talked to several people, many of whom were on a spiritual path like his own. Normally, he loved to discuss matters of the spirit with like-minded people, but today he found himself glancing toward the door each time it opened, to see who was arriving. Last weekend after the meditation, when they had all been invited to this potluck, Cathy had said she may come, but he had also heard her ask if spouses were invited. The answer from the host had been yes, if they can sit through the meditation. He really hoped she would come alone. He simply must talk to the one who had been on his mind all week.

"Anyone sitting here?"

Michael was abruptly brought back to the present, and smiled at a man he recognized from other gatherings. "No, not yet," he answered.

The room was starting to fill as everyone finished eating and found their places for the meditation. He realized that she probably wasn't coming, and settled into a casual conversation with the man next to him. That was when she walked through the door. Alone. Their eyes met briefly across the room, and his followed her as she went into the kitchen to greet the host. She was just as he had been seeing her in his mind's eye all week, including that glow, the vitality of life that sparkled about her. He looked around and noticed with glee that the only empty chair was next to him—he willed that no one would take it before she came back in. She got some food and walked over to sit next to him.

"Don't you work?" Cathy asked in a hushed tone, without so much as a hello. She sat down.

"What?"

"I mean, were you thinking about me all week, or what? I have to work even if you don't!" She didn't know what else to say, and genuinely wondered how anyone could be so telepathically tuned in to her.

He was rather taken aback, but also intrigued. He answered, "Well, I didn't have much work this week, as a matter of fact. And yes, I have been thinking about you. How did you know?"

"I know."

He felt goosebumps on his back and arms. "Can we talk alone after this is over—maybe take a walk or something?" He tried not to sound like he was pleading, but the need to talk was overwhelming him.

She sighed, knowing that it would be against her marriage ethics to take a walk alone with this man, but the words were out before she could censor them. "All right."

He relaxed, and they said no more as the group meditation started. He found it difficult to concentrate, because he was planning out where they would go, and all he wanted to say to her. She was wondering how she could possibly make this OK to herself and husband, but at the same time knew she couldn't say no. The pull was too strong, and she had to find out why.

They left shortly after the meditation, saying good byes to their friends separately. Once outside, he suggested they each drive and meet down at the beach. She agreed, even though it was raining fairly steadily now and she remembered that she had no rain clothes with her. She followed his truck down the curvy road and parked in the empty parking lot.

They got out of their cars and walked silently toward the water through the thick sand. The beach was windy and cool. He tentatively put his arm around her shoulders and, though there was a tiny voice inside that resisted, she didn't pull away. It felt so perfectly natural, and she had stopped being surprised anymore as she accepted the situation and her own reactions.

"Well, what is going on here? You know I am married," she began.

"Yes, I know. And I don't know what's going on any more than you do."

"It's not OK with me to be alone with you," she declared.

He nodded in acknowledgment, but said nothing, and they continued to walk.

"I've been thinking about you all week," she continued, "and it is interfering with my work. I can't seem to concentrate. I'm a scientist, you know, and my work is highly mental. We have to do something about this."

"I've been having trouble concentrating also. We obviously have a really strong connection; maybe we can be spiritual partners in the inner planes. Maybe we can be just friends."

He said it, but couldn't really imagine that scenario. There was such a yearning he was feeling for her. He tried to analyze it—was this a sexual attraction? Was it just lust? After all, he had been alone for several years. No, this was a love so deep that it was his *soul* that was doing the yearning, not his loins. His heart was joyous just being next to her.

"I kinda feel like this is more of a man-woman thing, not just a friendship," she observed glumly. "I WANT to feel you mostly here," she put her hand on her heart, "rather than HERE." She pointed to her abdomen, where she could feel the Golden Cord in high activation. She was feeling most of this pull between them along the cord between their navels, even though she knew that the connection was at many levels.

He was surprised at her boldness and pondered what she had said for a few minutes, not really understanding it but not wanting to ask any more about it. It was comfortable being together even in silence, though there was a tension, an attraction that was hard to ignore. Dodging the occasional surges of waves, they meandered slowly along the shore in the wet sand just above the water. The rain was light but steady, the wind blowing it strongly against them. They made some small talk about the beach and surroundings. Michael had an umbrella and tried to hold it in front of Cathy in the driving rain. Appreciating the gesture, she said she would rather see where she was going than be dry. The wild weather suited her on what seemed like a wild adventure, and she had always loved rain.

Cathy stopped to take her shoes off, saying that she wanted to feel the sand directly on her bare feet, an act that amazed Michael because of the icy temperature of the sand. Already accepting the fact that they might somehow get together—that she was his soulmate—he suddenly wondered if she was too much younger than he.

As she removed her socks and tucked them into her running shoes, he casually asked, "So what is your astrological sign? When is your birthday?"

She told him the date, including the year. "Lots of energy in Gemini. And yours?"

"Cancer-Leo cusp, in July."

She noted that he didn't tell her the year he was born, and surmised that he must be sensitive about his age. *It doesn't matter, because we are just friends,* she told herself firmly, *and besides, he couldn't be older than my husband.* Mike was eleven years her senior and it was not a problem because his body was in good shape. She assessed the shape of Michael's body, remembering that he was a soccer coach, and saw that he, too, was fit—then she realized what she was doing and dismissed the train of thought as irrelevant.

After they had walked about half a mile, Michael suggested they head back. They turned toward each other for just a moment and before either of them knew what was happening, they were locked in an embrace, as if the wind had suddenly swept in from both sides and pushed them together.

Immediately, all their chakras started activating, spinning wildly as they interacted in feedback loops, resonating into a swirl of energy. They were lifted up by this surge of power, up into the cosmos, where they soared together among the stars, far above the planet, flowing with the cosmic currents. Their spirits were finally free. Flying together in joyful bliss, they knew without a doubt that they were perfect companions in spirit. Instantly they knew that, after a very, very, long journey, they were two souls who had finally come home. They felt like they had finally found that part of themselves that they had long missed, and they were filled with bliss, forgetting all else.

The universe seemed to celebrate with them, as angels and countless other Beings of Light surrounded them with song and beautiful displays of color. It all happened in a moment, yet the moment was timeless. The Golden Cord between them was taken to an even higher level of activation, as if it had been waiting for this moment for an eternity, sealing their energy together—and right then nothing in the outside world mattered as long as they were together.

When they settled back into their bodies, neither could say anything but "Wow." When they looked into each other's eyes, they could see that it was a mutual experience.

Cathy came to her senses and gently pulled away, and they slowly started walking back. *What just happened?* She wondered silently. *Is that what it is like to hug your soulmate? I can only call it Heaven.*

"That was like heaven." He tentatively whispered.

"Yes, pretty amazing. I was just thinking that very word." Their telepathic connection was growing even stronger.

The wind was at their backs now, and the rain had relaxed into a light sprinkle, so it was easier going. They walked in silence for a few minutes, both thinking about soulmates and knowing now, after that hug, that they had never been with one before. It was not something either of them wanted to talk about yet, however, and they didn't have words for it even if they did want to, so they discussed other spiritual experiences they had each had, finding commonalties.

They found that they shared the idea that when human beings spiritually evolve so they are no longer personality-based but live their lives centered in the soul instead, it became appropriate to change their name to more accurately reflect their true essence. Michael revealed that he had already been given his spiritual name during meditation.

"Tell me how you got it," she urged.

"I sat in meditation and opened my crown chakra, slowly bringing in golden and white Light until my body was completely filled, and it started radiating outward, filling my Light body. Then I simply asked for my spiritual name. The Light immediately changed to a deep emerald green color, and I heard 'OMARAN' loudly spoken, clear and strong. It was an amazing experience."

"That is a great name! Why don't you use it?" She was impressed.

"I guess I'm not ready for that. I've lived and done business in this county for almost twenty years, and everyone knows me as Michael. Do you think I should?"

"I think I'd like to call you Omaran from now on. It suits you, and it brings out your highest and best qualities."

"OK, I'd like that. What about you? Do you have a spiritual name yet?"

"No, I have never even asked for it, though I've always disliked my given name. 'Cathy' never did suit me, even as a child, and I cringe inside slightly every time people call me that. I've been wanting to change it all my life but never settled on the right name."

"Didn't you say that you can communicate with your spirit guides? Maybe it is time to ask them."

"Yes, maybe it is time. Out of respect, I don't ask them anything unless I consider it to be important, and worth their time and effort."

She said it like channeling was a common ability, but Michael knew of few people who had that talent. He was very interested in this, because he had once taken a channeling workshop and was successful during the class, but he hadn't stuck with it and now felt he had some blocked energy around it. Though he talked to his guides often, and felt their presence, he didn't get answers back directly. He wanted to know more.

"How did you learn how to channel, anyway?"

She described how she had always felt close to her spirit guides since her first real contact at a very young age, and had communicated with them intuitively until she was in her early thirties. Then one day it just occurred to her to let them talk through her aloud. She had gotten books on channeling and researched the process, and started practicing, little by little getting the connection stronger until she could get out of the way enough so they could speak, while she remained fully present and acted like a translator. Then she practiced whenever she could, getting advice from them for herself mainly, and once in a while doing a reading for others.

"Most of the time I just communicate with them telepathically, without verbal channeling. They call themselves the Council of Seven. They are so loving, compassionate, and wonderful—it is my own personal support group. Their primary purpose is to help me grow and evolve in this lifetime, and I've learned so much from them."

"And have you asked them about us?" He immediately wished he hadn't blurted that out so soon, but there it was.

She had been hesitant about asking her guides about him in much detail, because she was a bit afraid of what they might say. She answered, "I only asked whether it was in the highest good to see you, and the answer was affirmative, which is the reason I am here now."

In the highest good to see me! He thought. This was encouraging, and validating. He said, "It must be nice to have that connection . . . to have a two-way conversation with wise beings who can see so much more than we humans can. Do they look like angels to you?"

"Yes, sometimes I call them angels, or spirit guides. I really appreciate them—they are my best friends."

"Do they tell you what to do, or give you warnings? Do they protect you?" Omaran really wondered what it was like to have living contact with the "other side."

She smiled. "No, they never tell me what to do. Beings of the Light don't do that. If people have guides telling them what to do or trying to control them in some way, those are not beings of the Light, and don't have the higher purpose of the person in mind. My guides certainly give advice, but usually only when I ask for it, and even then, they never interfere with my learning process or decisions. They are not allowed to interfere in any way."

"What about telling you the future? Do they do that?"

"Very rarely. I've asked about some things, of course . . . who wouldn't? And they patiently told me that they are not fortunetellers, because giving that kind of knowledge might influence the outcome of situations, and doesn't help the person evolve spiritually. They do, on occasion, bring my attention to something I may not have noticed, or let me know about things that might happen, that kind of thing. But if I have a decision to make, for example, they don't tell me how to make it, but instead they guide me through a process to help me see which choice has the most Light, or something like that. They have guided me through many things this way, taught me basic lessons in spirituality, and given me many tools and much knowledge. I guess it is similar to having a guru, like in the Hindu tradition, but in spirit, rather than in body."

"That is really fascinating. I wish I could communicate with mine like that." He really envied this skill.

"I believe that everyone gets what they need, when they need it, so if you needed that you would have it, or be drawn to spend time developing it." She looked at him meaningfully. "You know, I've never talked to anyone about this so much, except with my sisters, of course. I've always kept it fairly private."

They were arriving back at the parking lot, and Michael asked if he could call her.

"No, I don't think that is a good idea."

"Well, then, will you be going to the group meditation next weekend?"

"Maybe, I'll have to see. I need time to think. I'll call you if I am going."

She started to edge away, feeling suddenly uncomfortable. He took out a business card with his phone number on it and stepped close to give it to her. Just before they parted, he impulsively and quickly kissed her on the lips, two light pecks.

Startled, Cathy's knees weakened, almost buckling beneath her. She blushed, and recovered her balance quickly, turning toward her car. She fumbled with the key but managed to get in and then proceeded to turn the wrong way in the large parking lot, right into a dead end. Flustered, she turned around and followed his waiting truck out to the road, knowing that he must have found that very amusing. She was right.

Three

In the night it seems,
you ride throughout my dreams,
you're there until I try to hold you.
Just barely out of reach,
it's madness as we hide and seek,
you are the breath of me,
I must have you.

> — From the song
> "Only in My Dreams"

All week Cathy was again preoccupied with thoughts of Michael/ Omaran, and he of her. On Thursday, she got up the courage to call him and they arranged to meet at his apartment and go to the meditation that weekend together. He was ecstatic, and a bit nervous. Was this sort-of like a date?

She told herself, *It is not technically lying to Mike when I tell him I'm going to a meditation group.* But she was withholding information and she didn't like that. She had always been so loyal, so honest. She just needed to be absolutely sure about what was happening before telling him.

She arrived in time to get a quick look at Omaran's apartment, then they both got in Tan Man, his truck. As they were driving over, the reality of the situation struck her: she was, in some way, getting involved with a highly spiritual man who drove a well-used truck, did construction work, and lived in a mediocre apartment. Why didn't he own a house at his age? Obviously he didn't have it together financially! Her husband and she were both scientists and monetarily comfortable. *Why in the world am I here? What am I getting into? This is absurd!*

After the event, they arrived back at his apartment and she went directly to her little blue Toyota, which she called Zippy.

"Won't you come in for some tea or something?" he asked hopefully.

"I don't think so . . . I really need to get home to my family." That was certainly true, but what she didn't say was that a passion was growing in her the strength of which she had never felt for any man. And she definitely did not want to become involved romantically before telling her husband about this. That was the least (and the best) she could do. She didn't want to be in a situation where she could be tempted.

Omaran asked, "Then will I see you next weekend? How about going on a hike or something?" *I can't let her go without a plan to meet again,* he thought. Over the course of the evening, he had been running through many scenarios in his mind, and a hike seemed most appealing, away from other people, just the two of them. . . .

She hesitated. "Maybe. I'll call you to confirm after I see what my kids and Mike have planned."

She felt immediate guilt with that thought, and quickly got into Zippy. He nodded, and closed the door for her. She rolled down the window just enough to hear him say good night, and their eyes met. In that look, their human forms slipped away, and their souls' eternal closeness was almost tangible—as if they were looking into a mirror that reflected back not only their own form, but their combined beingness. It was a look they would both remember.

The times between talks on the phone seemed like little pieces of eternity the next week for Omaran. She called on Tuesday afternoon, and they had a brief but hardly satisfying conversation. Though Omaran really did not know how all of this would turn out, he was now absolutely certain that Cathy was his soulmate. He longed to be with her more, to at least talk to her on the phone daily, but it couldn't happen, at least not yet.

He was suddenly having a strong urge to spend time at his piano, for he was hearing beautiful songs about their union coming through him that he was compelled to write down. They weren't just love songs. He was convinced that they were divinely inspired, as the words flowed through him in a way he had never before experienced. He had been a songwriter/singer for most of his life, but these were different. The words expressed much more than he himself really understood. He could hardly wait to share them with her.

Waiting until the next weekend was such a challenge! He wondered if all soulmates felt like this when they met. Was this intense energy pulling them together normal? And all they had done was hug! He wrote a letter to her, expressing what he could not say.

> *Angel,*
>
> *And so, my lovely, a letter of "I don't knows!" I don't know if I'll finish it; I don't know if I'll give it to you if I do (I suspect I will); I don't know how much of what I want to say I'll really say.*
>
> *The energy feels different today—not as frantic; still, certainly, just as sure, just as knowing! Perhaps I should have known, I was warned. The universe said, "Ask, but be specific." Some things didn't matter to me, but I missed one big part. It never occurred to me that I had to include "Let her be available."*
>
> *I'm not in shock, more like disbelief. It's hard to accept that we won't be together for a while longer. At one point I thought it would probably be easier not to see you any more—I'm still not sure how I feel about that. On the other hand, it is a great comfort to me that I have found you.*
>
> *The last time we talked on the phone, I told you about the deep, deep loneliness that I used to sometimes feel. A large part of it was from missing my spiritual family— but an even larger part was missing the other half of me. When we talked I didn't feel comfortable in adding that part. Now, there is nothing I would keep from you.*
>
> *In the calm of my mind today, among other things, I remembered saying many times in the past, "The next*

time I'm with someone, she will have to be The One!"
Although recently, in the last few months, I'd been giving
that up. Letting go. Thinking, she may not even be on
the planet. I can let all that go now. Again, the universe
is surprising me. This is not what I expected, or thought
would happen.

I feel you when I feel you. I'm quite sure you go to
bed sooner than I. I will think of you more at night, when
you're asleep, than when you're awake, because when I
think of you it distracts you at work.

She beheld him—the White Knight . . .
but he appeared on a pale horse.
He found her, the lost princess . . .
but she was temporarily in a too-tall tower.
And so he withdrew a ways.

Sweet dreams my lovely!
O.

When she had time alone to meditate, Cathy tried to analyze the
flame that was ignited inside her, a passionate flame that she knew only
Omaran could satisfy. The Golden Cord had become larger and more
tangible, more and more accepted as part of her energy field, as though
it had always been there, just waiting to be activated. She felt at times
almost tortured because she was still trying to fight against the force
pulling her to him, even though she intuitively knew that it was no use.
Giving in to the pull would force her to make big changes in her life, and
be difficult to explain to anyone, most of all her husband and two sons.

Her life was comfortable. She loved Mike and he loved her. The
resistance she felt to seeing her world crumble and rebuild itself caused
her great strain. When she channeled, her guides kept telling her to keep
her heart open, and to have faith that all would work out for the best for
everyone involved, and this sustained her.

They had also told her that Omaran was her twin flame, and that
the two of them were drawn together now for a purpose. She didn't

really understand what twin flames were, and how they differed from soulmates, except that she only had one twin flame or twin soul but many soulmates. She supposed that made him quite special, and it did explain the unusual connections they had, but was she expected to just drop everything in her life to be with him? What kind of a plan was this?

On Wednesday evening, Cathy was getting ready to meditate, sitting alone in her bedroom on the edge of the queen-sized bed. She knew she wouldn't be disturbed because of her bright yellow posterboard sign with a string attached that was slung over the doorknob that said, "IN MEDITATION - Please don't disturb except for emergencies. Thanks!" It had been a wonderful idea to make the sign, because before, the kids or Mike would knock for every little thing that came up. Now they knew she would be out in 30-45 minutes and it certainly had not hampered the family that she spent this time alone every evening. Things could wait.

She first pulled out her round Mother Peace tarot cards, and did a quick reading pertaining to her relationship with Omaran. The final outcome was the Death card. She stared for a while at the picture of a snake shedding its skin, sighed, and put them away. She knew that the card meant a shedding of the old to make way for the new—a major transformation, change, a new person.

She settled into her meditation posture, closed her eyes, and asked her guides and ascended masters to help her make the changes quickly and easily, to be reborn and not resist the changes. An intense transformative experience overtook her. She was suddenly surrounded by angels and masters, who obviously had some kind of intent. They got her immediate, undivided attention. This was different from the usual contact she had with these beings, and over the years she had come to recognize these kinds of events as initiations, always taking her by surprise and turning a normal meditation into an orchestrated ceremony in the higher realms.

Their energy quickly swept her into the inner planes where they were. The love and support all around her was very tangible. One radiant being came forward and she realized that it was Master Jesus. Though she had glimpsed him at a distance, with other Light beings and angels, she did not consciously remember ever seeing Jesus this close up before.

He glowed with warmth and love, combined with power and strong intent, as she looked into his eyes.

He smiled and said softly into her mind, "Beloved one, we want to show you something."

She nodded and watched as a magnificent being of Light appeared above her, so bright that she could hardly look at it directly. The energy from this being seemed familiar, and there was a sense of great joy within herself and emanating from the being. She looked questioningly toward Jesus.

He looked directly into her eyes and said, "This is you. This is your Divine Presence, the real you."

She gasped in disbelief, and looked more closely at the bright Light. It did resemble her in a vague way. Before she realized what was happening, she suddenly found herself merged with the being, and filled with such Light that she had doubts she could contain it. She looked down, and saw that she was wearing a long, flowing, white robe that shined with a Light of its own. It felt wonderful, like she was made entirely of Light.

Then something felt strange between her shoulder blades, a stirring, and wings started growing out of them! Huge wings! She was suddenly impacted with the thought that she had been longing to get her wings back for a long, long time and didn't even know it until this moment— in fact she didn't even know she had wings until now! Tears welled up and flowed out freely, as a deep pain surfaced, combining with the immense joy.

"If this is me, why didn't I know until now?" She demanded. "Why did I have to go through so much suffering and pain all that time? If I had known that I had such Light, it wouldn't have been so hard!"

The sobs grew stronger as the release and reality of it sank in. She didn't expect an answer, and didn't get one. The masters surrounded her with their love and support and let her release her eons of frustration, of longing for this union, of putting herself through untold pain in incarnation after incarnation, of missing that which she couldn't name. She cried for half an hour, then felt as though a tremendous weight had been lifted. It was such a relief to know that she really was a Light being! And that she had wings, like an angel!

The joy overcame her and she was finally able to enjoy sitting with her Higher Presence, absorbing as much of her source energy as she could, so she could remember it when she came back to normal consciousness.

"Omaran, I have to tell you about something that happened last night!" She was so glad to finally have someone to talk to about her spiritual experiences, someone who listened and even seemed to understand. Though she hadn't known him long, she felt like she had known him forever, and could share anything. Sitting at the dining room table, she shifted the phone to the other ear. She had just gotten home from work and the kids were busy out in the yard, so she took advantage of a moment alone before Mike got home.

"What? Tell me."

"In a meditation last night, I was taken through an intense initiation in which I merged with my Higher Presence. I saw that part of me clearly for the first time! Jesus was there. Plus—maybe you won't believe this, but—I found out I have wings! Big ones!" She could still feel them between her shoulder blades, and they felt natural. If she closed her eyes she could see them clearly.

"No kidding! Wow. That is great, congratulations! And what a coincidence!"

"What?"

"Well, a couple of days ago I got my wings back!" He was astounded by yet another parallel in their spiritual unfoldment.

"Really? That's pretty unbelievable," she said.

"Tell me about your experience first."

She shared her experience in as much detail as she could remember, and he listened.

"Wow, that is so fantastic," he said. "And the wings part is amazingly like what I experienced, though I had asked for them first. Last weekend I had just finished reading Solara's book, *Star Borne*, and she talks about how it is time for all angels who incarnated to find their wings again and their true natures. You should read it, it will help you understand the process."

"I will get it right away."

"So I decided to see if I could experience my wings, or if I had them at all. It was late morning, and I was in the lower bedroom, which doesn't have much natural light. I stood up with eyes closed, and said out loud, 'If I have wings, please show me a sign!'

"All of a sudden, the light began getting brighter and brighter, until even with my eyes closed it was almost blinding. I began weeping from pure joy, and I felt my body release as if the tension was just melting away. And then—I saw and felt my wings. I cried even more, but oh! such joy. I have wings!"

Cathy said, "That is really neat. But I never thought angels really had wings. I thought that was just a way they were depicted by artists in paintings, like maybe the wings are symbolic of their purity and divinity, or of being messengers of the Divine."

"Yeah, it is interesting. I only know what I experienced, and that I can still feel my own wings."

It was one of a series of influential events that had occurred at about the same time to each of them, even before they had met, such as reading certain influential books at the same times. The more they talked, the more of these "coincidences" they discovered in their past.

She came to call this event "Awakening to my Angel Self," and the next day, bought the book that Omaran had suggested and started reading it. There she found her experience described and explained, and was comforted by the fact that others had apparently experienced a similar thing. The book said that all angels needed to awaken now. It also described how they are different from most of the people on the planet, and had a hard time fitting in.

She had always felt different, and had assumed it was because she had been on the planet for so much longer than most others—she often thought she had experienced everything this place could offer, many times over, and that there was nothing new to learn. She could remember many of her lives, in bits and pieces, and knew she had many times gone against the moral or societal norms of the time, to follow instead what she believed in—which had gotten her into a lot of trouble, and killed many times.

But perhaps it wasn't only her advanced soul age that made her different, after all. Her energy make-up was also different. She had figured out as a child that her energy vibrated at a different frequency or level than most others, and that this had a catalytic effect on many people, pushing them to heal or change whatever they were not addressing in their lives. Just by being around her, she had noticed people undergoing big transformations, as if she "stirred them up." Now she wondered whether this quality of inducing growth was due to her spiritual lineage.

Four

Cathy and Omaran met in a parking lot on Mt. Tamalpais that Saturday to take one of Omaran's favorite hikes. He pointed her to the trail, letting her lead. He found that he really liked following her, watching her walk and seeing that she marveled at the same beautiful things he did. He was glad that she was so at home in the woods, so sure-footed as she agilely made her way along the trail.

They found that hiking in natural environments was one thing they shared a passion for, and Omaran loved showing her one of his favorite trails on the mountain. Mostly silent as they walked, they felt a deep reverence, taking in the beauty in the surrounding forest, with its lush greenery, deep, dark soil, and creeks flowing plentifully across the path. Such richness provided replenishment for all the senses and the soul, which was so needed in this time of stress and uncertainty.

They were drawn to a thick grove of redwoods off to the side of the trail, so they detoured to it and lay on their backs next to each other to look up at the giants. The redwood branches made a canopy above them in a pattern that looked like a mandala, and they stared up at it.

"I started writing a song about us." Omaran casually remarked.

"About us? I'd like to hear it."

He hummed a few lines, but couldn't remember much. "I'll play it for you if you come back to my apartment."

"I think I'd better go home directly. I don't want my family to miss me too much." She was thinking that her strongest urge right then was to roll over and lie on top of him. The yearning inside her womb was getting stronger each time she saw him—in her *womb,* of all places! How could anyone attract her like this? What was it about him? Being near him made her feel so complete, so much at home, and she wanted to get closer—a lot closer. But at the expense of her marriage? She could feel the sparks fly when they touched, and wondered if she was going to be able to wait. Just how strong was her control, anyway?

"Do you know how much I love you?" He rolled to one side, propped up onto one elbow. "I have waited for you all my life."

She allowed his words to temporarily soothe her growing anxiety. He was so sincere. She smiled. "Well, you were married before, I don't call that waiting."

He laughed. "Well, except for that." She could be witty at times, and he enjoyed that.

She wistfully commented, "Too bad we couldn't have met twenty years ago."

"I wouldn't have been ready for you twenty years ago. You probably wouldn't have liked me then, and our age difference would have been too much," he replied. He had revealed the week before that he was twelve years older than she was, and at this time in their lives it didn't matter to either of them.

She looked back up at the canopy and said, "You're probably right, but meeting at this time in our lives isn't exactly convenient. Do you think we set this up long ago, or did it just happen?" She sighed and thought, *Why does it have to be so complicated? Why would my Higher*

Self arrange such an impossible situation in which to finally bring my long-lost soulmate into my life?

"I can't answer that. It does seem like bad timing, but I also have faith in the right timing of the universe, so somehow it will end up for the higher good, whether we are able to be together now or not."

Omaran instantly regretted saying that last part because he didn't really want to consider that they may not get together somehow. He knew it must be tearing her apart inside. She was obviously a good person and didn't want to hurt her husband. But though at times over the last few weeks he had thought it best to stop seeing each other, he knew that he simply couldn't do it—any more than he could voluntarily stop breathing.

He quickly changed the direction of the conversation before she could respond. "I wrote a letter to you a few days ago. If only we could talk more during the week, I'd be able to stand not seeing you until the next weekend. Read it when you get home, OK? Not now." He pulled out the folded yellow piece of paper from his pocket and gave it to her.

When she read his letter that evening several times, alone in the bedroom, it filled her with longing and renewed the conflict within her. She stashed it in the most private place she could think of, in her journal, and the secretiveness of it was almost unbearably uncomfortable. She was not a secretive person, and it went against her nature to be carrying on this way. How long could she stand it? She picked up a pen and a pad of paper.

> *Omaran,*
>
> *It's my turn to write—it seems like it has always helped me organize my thoughts and feelings. I'm just wondering if I've completely lost touch with reality, gone off the deep end. I've known you really only a couple of weeks, and in that time we've spent only a few hours together. It seems absurd that I could feel so deeply for you in such a short time. It's never happened to me before.*
>
> *I've been in love four times in this life. Each time it started as a friendship and slowly grew into romance. This*

is so different. Not only in how quickly it is developing, but in its intensity. The baud rate (sorry—computer jargon) and magnitude of the energy between us is astounding. When I'm in your arms I want nothing else. My womb yearns for you like I've never experienced. I don't just mean physically, more like all my bodies—physical, emotional, mental, and spiritual—want you. The fire in my belly gets bigger and hotter each time we touch. It's as if there's a resonance with you on all levels. My desire for you is an order of magnitude greater than any I've felt for other men. I thought I had felt passion! Ha!

Now that I've written all that, I really doubt that I'll be giving you this letter—I think I've revealed too much! But I feel better having put words to it. Maybe I'll be able to have more control now. I've always been very much in control of my actions and thoughts. This just isn't like me at all, but then I've never met anyone like you.

I really gave up on finding a man who was even close to me in spiritual development, probably thousands of years ago, come to think of it. Have I been missing you for that long? I read somewhere that as the Ascension draws near, people will find their twin flames if they are on the Earth. I asked my guides about that and they said you were mine! That we are twin flames and that is why the attraction is so strong. That we need to be together at this time in our evolution because we amplify each other's growth.

(No need to sign because I won't give this to him.)

She felt better after writing, and stashed it next to Omaran's letter. Up until a few weeks ago, she had written often in her journal, and wrote songs and poems to express herself. But now she was afraid to write anything, even though she knew Mike would never invade her privacy. Just this one time she had to write something, because it seemed like she would burst otherwise. What she was feeling could no longer be contained. She could not talk to anyone about it. She didn't dare, especially since she hadn't told Mike yet. Even her sisters, with whom she was close, didn't know. She had only her spirit guidance, which she appreciated, but it wasn't quite the same as telling someone in the flesh.

The next week was one of great soul-searching for Cathy. She felt just awful about what was happening, yet she knew that she couldn't stop it. The force was too great, and the pain she felt was not due to the force itself, but because of *resisting* it. Though she had been in love several times, she knew it was never like this. Never did she feel like she was on such a rip tide, out of her control. If she hadn't been married, it would have been extremely pleasant, and exciting. But in her current situation, it was ripping her to pieces as she resisted making the changes required to delve in and follow the currents, allowing them to take her as they would.

She was slowly beginning to grasp the possibility that she would go there whether she went willingly or not; that it was her fate, perhaps some kind of agreement her soul made eons ago that she may simply have to abide by. Deep in the recesses of her mind—almost conscious, but not entirely so—there seemed to be an agreement with Omaran that transcended all human form. She knew she had free will and could decide never to see him again, but there was a gnawing feeling that if she did that, he would turn up again in her life anyway. And that even if she could avoid him, she was imprinted, bonded to him at the soul and higher levels, a connection that she would not be able to ignore or easily live with, if they were apart.

But no matter how unavoidable it may be, it was happening so quickly that she just wasn't ready to make a decision yet that would cause so much pain to her husband and kids, and upset her comfortable life. She spent more time than usual in the evenings alone in meditation, trying to make sense of her life. Mike didn't question it, but she thought he must surely know that something was up. Several times she drew a tarot card about the situation, and got The Tower, an image of disaster, the burning destruction of all forms . . . the great Kali, creator and destroyer of things, working in her own life; the giving up of all that is stable and the reorganization into a new and better life. *Oh my,* she thought.

Her guides lovingly supported her whenever she tuned to them. They answered the questions in her mind as best they could, being neutral and careful not to influence her decisions. Their advice, as always, was full of love and understanding, giving her information that might help, but honoring her free will.

Five

I looked for you in love,
I looked for you in pain,
I looked for you in laughter,
I looked for you in vain.
Every eye that I would catch
I'd wonder, is it you?
Searching faces for your smile
looking for a clue.

— From the song
"Twin Flames"

Dear One,

I call your name silently many times. Mostly, your Earth name. Even if you can't hear it, I know you feel it. And besides, it makes me feel good—it's almost like talking to you. The last two days have been amazing. It seems like so much has happened. I'm sure I'll tell you about it when we talk, but I wanted to write it down.

I mentioned that sometime last week I had started a new melody. Well, Saturday night, words began to come. It seems this song will be about twin flames—imagine that! Some time Sunday morning, in meditation, I saw a scene of us long ago, just at the time this planet was about to become peopled. The feeling I got was that we knew we would be apart most of the time, but we vowed

to be together again when the planet rose toward Light
and Life. I almost feel or think that I am beginning to
remember. I love you so much!

One more thing. I truly hope that one time, before we
leave this dimension, we can feel each other completely.
We will meet again in the stars—we will dance there . . .
and the angels won't be able to tell us apart!

Love, Always and in All Ways,
O.

C athy put the letter down and sighed. He certainly had a way with words, a way of wedging himself into her heart. They were sitting next to a small waterfall as she read the letter Omaran had written earlier that week. She stared at the water as it cascaded over the rocks, and breathed in the moist air charged with negative ions.

They had met on Mt. Tamalpais again, for a short hike after she had spent most of the day in the woods alone, in meditation. It wasn't long enough for her to get completely clear about her situation, but it had certainly helped. She had to get clear and fast, because this just couldn't go on as it was much longer. She had to tell Mike soon, and face the consequences of her actions.

Omaran knew many lovely hikes. Walking with him in the woods reminded her of a poem she had written as a teenager, about her perfect love and partner, and how it was going to be when they found each other, walking in the woods together. She had long ago given up finding him, considering it a fantasy of childhood, and here she was, middle-aged and many relationships later, coming face-to-face with the very one she had written about—but a little late!

She said, "So you think we are twin flames? Do you know what that means?" She wondered how he could be writing a song about it, how he could be sure. She wasn't even sure that she believed they were twin flames, and her guides had told her so directly!

"I think it means that when the soul is born, or first differentiates from God, it is born as a pair. Like two halves of a whole. Same as twin souls, but more rare than soulmates. It feels like that is what we are, doesn't it? Why don't you ask your guides?" He took a deep breath of the clean March air.

"I did."

"And?" He asked.

She hesitated. "They said we are."

He smiled, excited. "I thought so. Anything else?"

"Well, I asked about the difference between soulmates and twins. It seems that soulmates are all the beings we connect with on a soul level, and have been incarnating with over and over, through many dramas and experiences. We know them really well, like soul family, and when soulmates talk it is about deep issues, spiritual and philosophical stuff— issues that are important to the soul."

"That makes sense. So we can have several soulmates in our lives, in many kinds of relationships."

"Yes. And there is only one twin flame. They don't come together in incarnation very often, just at really important times—like the final lifetime, or to start something important, or during big changes on the planet."

"Sounds like this time definitely qualifies," he said.

"Yes, but for some reason, and my guides didn't tell me why, most who incarnate together don't stay together for long. Maybe it is too intense. Most twin flames reunite with one of them acting as a spirit guide for the other, who is incarnated."

"Aha, so that makes us pretty special, doesn't it?" He moved closer. "Did your guides say anything else about us?"

"Yes, a lot, but I don't want to tell you yet." She edged away a bit, finding another uncomfortable position on the large boulder. "I'm still processing everything. This whole thing has been very difficult for me, you know."

"I know."

They were silent for a few minutes as they watched the falling water slowly and patiently erode the rocks away, grain by grain. Shadows of the bushes and trees flickered in patterns on the ground in the gentle breeze.

He decided to tell her. "I had a vision of us in a meditation, a memory that I didn't write about in that letter," he began, very softly, gazing into the distance. "It was a long time ago, right after I was first made aware of myself as an individual being, like I had just been born as a spirit. I was sort-of like out in space, and I opened my eyes for the first time. As I became fully conscious of myself as a being, I was aware of another presence right by my side. And guess what—I turned and there you were beside me, just opening your eyes for the first time, too. Don't ask me how I knew it was you—it was your essence. I cried for the joy of it."

"Wow. So that's why you think we are twin flames?"

"I don't think. I just know."

"Hmmm . . . well, just because we are cosmic mates doesn't necessarily mean that it is right for us to be together now. We should have met ten years ago! I'm married, and I'm not willing to just have an affair with you. Is that what you want?"

He wondered how she could possibly think that was all he wanted. He assured her, "What I want is for you to leave your husband and be with me. I don't think it is any accident that we came together now, and maybe it is selfish of me, but I have looked for you all my life and I want to be with you however we can do it. I think we have been brought together by Spirit, and who are we to question the timing?"

"That is easy for you to say—you are single. I have to give up a lot to be with you, on faith alone. It is happening much too fast."

He leaned closer and spoke quietly, looking directly into her eyes. "You are right. This is much harder for you than for me because of our situations. But I am absolutely certain that we are soulmates, at least, if not twin flames. And look at what has happened to bring us together. I love you at a depth I have never loved anyone before. I would do anything for you. I think you feel the same for me."

She felt like she was being swept away by his love and devotion.

As he continued, he felt a surge of energy coming through him. "I will commit to you at whatever level you want. We will marry as soon as you are free. I will love you forever. Please say you will be with me."

She wanted to fall into his arms and stay there for eternity . . . but her last trickle of restraint held firm and she didn't give in, for her husband's sake. Instead she quietly declared, "I will tell Mike tomorrow."

Six

I will take you there,
out among the stars,
the angel wings are ours.
I will take you there,
where it all began,
come take my hand.

— From the song
"I Will Take You There"

"Mike, we have to talk."
It was Sunday and Cathy's sons were out with friends for the day, so she and Mike had the house to themselves. It was time. Mike picked up on her nervousness, and knew that it was something important. She hadn't been her affectionate self lately, avoiding him all week. He wanted to know what was going on, but a part of him was afraid of the answer. They sat on the couch in their living room, facing each other.

She looked at her husband of seven years, and a sense of appreciation and love overtook her. A handsome man, even now that his sandy-colored hair was thinning on top, he had a tall, muscular body, reflective of his being raised on a dairy farm in the Midwest. He was a good husband and stepdad to her kids, and she didn't want to hurt hum. She hesitated for only a moment.

"I have something important to tell you."

"OK . . . what?" His face was flushed in anticipation.

Never one to beat around the bush, she dropped the bombshell, "I found my soulmate and I want to be with him."

There, she had said it. Mike was shocked. He always thought they would be together for the rest of their lives, and this just did not register.

"What do you mean, your soulmate?"

"Well, I met him at a meditation seminar and I know he is my soulmate and we need to be together. I don't want to hurt you, but the attraction is so strong I can't stop it." She didn't want to mention twin flames. That was too much to bring up all at once.

"Who is he? Where does he live? Do I know him?"

"He lives in Marin, and you don't know him."

"Yeah, I've heard about the people in Marin, and their loose morals. How dare he go for a married woman? Tell me his name, I'll look him up! I'm not giving you up that easily! Who does he think he is?"

She could see the anger flaring in him, which she had expected. Mike didn't get angry easily, he was a kind soul, but this was really threatening him. She felt awful.

"I don't want to give you his name yet."

"Have you slept with him?"

"No, I couldn't do that to you . . ." She was very glad she could say that honestly. ". . . but I want to."

Mike closed his eyes and took a couple of deep breaths. Using his Zen meditation skills to center himself, he sat up straighter and shook his whole body to release the tension. He consciously decided to look at it from a different perspective before his anger got out of control.

She waited, gazing out the large picture window behind Mike, to the unusual tree in the front yard, which the kids had dubbed the "puff-ball" tree, since they had not been able to properly identify its name. The tree was in full bloom, with large, white seedpods like giant dandelion tufts all over it. Looking at the tree relaxed her, and she felt Mike's tension slowly easing as well.

After five minutes of silence and integration, he finally said, "All right . . . all right . . . so now there are three of us, and we will figure out what to do with this new situation together. We are adults, and this is the 90s. We don't necessarily have to separate."

"But I want to be with him instead of you. He gives me spiritual sustenance that I really want."

"Something I couldn't give you . . . but you are happy with me in other ways, aren't you?"

"Well, yes."

"Then let's not act too quickly. What about your sons?"

This was another difficult subject. She had already put her sons through a divorce from their birth father, and she really dreaded telling them about this. They had accepted Mike as their stepfather. Even though they were no longer children, she knew it would be hard for them.

"I haven't told them yet, of course, and I don't plan on telling them until it is absolutely necessary. We need to work this through ourselves first."

"OK, that is good."

They talked for about an hour, and Mike allowed his emotions to range from anger to resignation to grief. He cried freely and so did she. When there was nothing more to say at that time, he announced, to her amazement, "I think I'll go into the bedroom and channel."

She nodded as she watched him walk down the hall and close the door. He had never channeled before, so she thought this may be interesting. Exhausted, she sat for a moment, calling in her guidance for help and support. *Am I doing the right thing?* She was too caught up in her own mental and emotional processes to get a clear answer, but she knew that her guides had been very positive, but gentle, about this new relationship. They had said that the Higher Plan was at work, and everyone, even Mike, would be better off in the end. She could hardly believe how fast events were happening—as if a huge wave had rolled in and she was riding it, along with Mike and Omaran.

When Mike came out of the bedroom about an hour later, he declared, "I talked to my guides and they told me to support you and your new man. I don't want to, but I know that I can either be a jerk about it, or I can be supportive, and my choice is to help you two get together because I now know that it is right."

She looked at him in awe. Obviously, Spirit was at work here big-time. She thought, *Mike suddenly awakened his ability to channel and his guides told him not only to let me go, but to help me? Wow. Unbelievable.*

"I really appreciate that," she said, feeling her heart open, and prickles on her skin.

"And I want to meet him right away."

"OK, I'll arrange it for next weekend if possible." She trusted Mike to be decent to Omaran, but she had no idea what would happen.

Mike spent the rest of the afternoon alone, taking a long walk then sitting in meditation in the bedroom, contemplating these new changes in his life. He had even surprised himself by the calm way he was handling this. Could he really just let her go to someone else? He knew intellectually that there was no stopping her when her mind was made up, but the terrible aching in his heart was almost too much to bear. It was his worst nightmare coming true, something he had never really considered possible. *What can I do now? Cathy loves someone else, and that is that. No changing that. But how to go on? All our plans. . . .*

He had never experienced a broken heart like this before. He had broken quite a few himself, but women had always been attracted to him, and fell in love with him easily. It was just part of his life. There was a magnetic quality about him that drew women, even now that he was over fifty. But this relationship with Cathy had been different, because for once he really wanted to be together for the rest of their lives. Deep down he knew this wasn't her fault, that the feelings of the heart cannot be chosen, but that didn't alleviate the pain. He would get through somehow. And maybe the whole thing would just turn out to be a fling, and she would come back. If that happened, he knew he would probably accept her back. His tears flowed freely as he thought about it.

In the evening, after Cathy and Mike retired to their room, they talked long into the night, as quietly as they could so the kids wouldn't hear. She felt an obligation to help him through his grief as much as she could, to make up for the pain she was causing him. His willingness to express his fears really impressed her—it was what she had hoped he would do someday, and here he was, using this crisis to unearth some of his deepest pain, pain he had been holding onto ever since she had known him. He allowed anything that came up to be immediately released in tears, laughter, shaking, and yawning, methods of release he was thankful he had learned years ago in Co-Counseling training.

Each night that week they spent hours together, working through deeper and deeper issues and pain. He freely told her everything he felt, and they grew closer as they worked through energy barriers that had been between them for years. She guided him through many insecurities and fears that came up, digging into his past to get at the core issues. He faced his worst fears head-on without reservation.

After several intense days, a transformation was becoming very apparent in Mike's energy field, and Cathy could see his heart chakra opening, as if layers of armor he had been shielding himself with had simply dissolved, allowing his heart to blossom like a flower in full bloom. Cathy was amazed that in less than one week he went through what most people would take years to heal—he was breaking through barriers she had always sensed in him, and finally revealing the real him. She loved him more than ever as she saw him quickly emerge into his potential by removing those blockages that had been in place for so long.

Mike also spent time every day talking to his spirit guides, who were very supportive and pleased to have a direct connection at last. He had known all along that if he ever really put his mind to it, he could channel them. It took a crisis, but he proved himself right. They told him clearly that even though it was painful now, it was best for him in the long run if he supported Cathy getting together with her new love, and didn't try to stop them. They also said he was very fortunate to be with Cathy because she was one of his spiritual teachers. He felt more love than ever for her, as his heart continued to open and he could finally express the appreciation and devotion that had eluded him before.

On Saturday afternoon, he and Cathy had the house to themselves and sat in the living room talking.

"So tomorrow's the big day," Mike said.

"You mean meeting Omaran? Yes, and I'm a bit nervous."

"Well, I'm actually looking forward to meeting him," he mused. He had gone through such an intense purging through the week, that he found he was now starting to accept the changes forced upon him—not only accept them, but embrace them without resistance! He amazed himself that he had been able to move through his pain so quickly, by simply embracing it and allowing it expression, and then come out the other end looking positively at his future.

"Looking forward to it?" She asked, surprised.

"Yes, and maybe we can even be friends," he declared. Friends! It was the first time he had considered this possibility, and he knew it to be true because his heart opened even more as he thought about it. He continued, "Well, from what you have told me about him, I already feel kinda close to the guy—after all, we both love the same woman. And if you love him, he has to be very special, or you would not have done something so drastic as breaking up our marriage."

Tears flowed freely down his cheeks for a minute, and he did not try to stop them. He reached for his handkerchief and blew his nose, wiped his eyes, then laughed and continued talking as if there had been no interruption.

"Anyway, I have a feeling that he and I are linked at a soul level, so I am now looking forward to our association, in whatever form it may take." He wondered what Omaran looked like, but didn't ask, and planned what he would say to him when they met.

When Omaran heard about how well breaking the news to Mike had gone, he was relieved to have that big step behind them, and very surprised that it had gone so smoothly. Cathy's guides had said all would be fine, but it was still hard to believe. Mike suddenly started channeling and his guides said to support them? It was almost too good to be true. He was suddenly apprehensive about meeting him.

As the week passed, he went through the anticipated meeting in his mind over and over again, trying out different scenarios and things to say. He wondered what Mike looked like. What sort of man could accept so quickly a change in his life that was this painful, and even want to have a cordial meeting with the "other man?" What an extraordinary man to be so understanding. He must have a heart of gold, and love Cathy very much. Omaran knew that he, himself, would not have taken it so well in a similar situation.

Maybe Mike was just pretending to be understanding and would catch him off guard, or maybe his anger just wouldn't come out until they met face to face. *I have to be prepared for anything,* Omaran thought.

But Cathy said that Mike was not the violent type, and he trusted her judgment. She wouldn't set up a meeting for the three of them if she didn't think it would go smoothly. And he reminded himself again that they had many angels looking after them, watching this whole drama and helping to surround them all with Divine love. Faith! He must have faith.

After attending a group meditation together on Sunday, Cathy and Omaran hiked to the place on Mt. Tamalpais where Mike had agreed to meet them. She had hiked this trail once before, through redwoods and ferns, one of her most favorite environments in the whole world. Talk was limited as they made their way through the forest, their minds mostly preoccupied with what was about to happen. When they finally reached the fire road, Mike watched them approach from a place where they couldn't see him, so he could get the first look, then he came out. The two men checked each other out briefly.

"Omaran."

"Mike."

Enough said. After a brief hesitation, the two men embraced awkwardly. Cathy breathed a sigh of relief, not realizing until then how nervous she had been.

"You want to hike or something?" Omaran pointed up the fire road.

"Sure," Mike said, "I looked earlier, and found a nice spot up ahead to sit with a view of the ocean."

Omaran replied, "Lead the way."

They hiked together on a lovely trail through the woods with glimpses of the ocean far below to their left, saying very little but exchanging large amounts of energy between them, the two men looking at each other as often as the situation permitted, analyzing each other's physical appearance and mannerisms. In a small meadow overlooking the sea, they stopped and sat on the grass and wild oats. There was a mild sea breeze, and the temperature was in the 70s, very comfortable.

As they sat in silence, looking out over the Pacific Ocean for a few moments and breathing in the clean, moist air, Omaran thought about all the things he had planned to say to Mike, but none of them came out smoothly now. He cleared his throat. "I just want to say that I am very grateful to you for being so understanding. I don't think I would be if I were in your position."

Mike smiled uneasily. "Thank you. It's not easy. I'm just taking it one day at a time. And my spirit guides advised me to support you guys, so that's what I'm going to do." For an instant, he tried to hold back the flood of tears, then gave in. He started sobbing. At first Omaran averted his eyes so as not to embarrass him, then his eyes got moist as well. Cathy wept too, and after a few minutes, Mike blew his nose on his bandana, and took a water jug out of his pack. They all took a sip, breathed deeply, and the tension was much eased between them.

This time, Cathy broke the silence. "Well, how about we meditate together and bring in Divine help to make this transition as smooth as possible?"

The two men agreed and made themselves comfortable. They sat in a triangle on the slope, the woman downhill facing up to the men, with her back to the sun and the sea. During the meditation, Cathy had a vision of the three of them sitting in a teepee together, long ago as Native Americans. When she shared this afterwards, they all felt a definite feeling of fate, a sense of the completion of some kind of agreement, or the finishing of a process started long ago between the three of them.

Cathy was absolutely relieved that the two men she loved were open to being friends, or at least to tolerating each other. The men talked for a long time, getting to know each other as she mostly watched and listened. More tears were shed. On the hike back, Mike wanted a picture of the three of them, so he solicited a passerby to shoot it with the camera he had brought, and the moment was captured in history.

Over the next few weeks, Mike continued to cry openly many times a day, releasing his grief as it came up, and Cathy supported him and listened to him. As Mike released, he felt lighter, his connection with his higher guidance grew stronger, and he spent more time in meditation and channeling. It was the beginning of a tremendous spiritual awakening. Now that he had been forced by circumstances through this period of fast growth, he looked back on his previous way of being and marveled that he had been holding on to so much pain for so long. Why hadn't he done this before? It felt so much better to go through it and be freed of it, rather than carrying it around! He wondered how many other people had pain they could release in the same way, and afterwards feel this much better.

Cathy watched the changes in Mike. She had never seen him or anyone else so willing to let go and cry. She often marveled at his open heart, and his ability to reach in and confront the pain. It was wonderful that he could stay so open and trusting of her, even after what she had done to him. That she could be there for him and help him through the process helped ease her guilt.

For many years she had longed for him to break through what she perceived as a sheath of emotional energy around him that kept him from really accessing his true feelings and spiritual abilities. The sheath had melted away quickly as he opened to the crisis and did not resist, allowing the energy to flow again. It was like a butterfly coming out of his cocoon at long last. She started to realize that this really was the best thing that could have happened to him. She understood more of what her guides had told her, about everyone being better off in the end, but she didn't tell him that until much later. *It is also rather ironic,* she thought, *that after telling him that I am leaving him for another, he is becoming more like the husband I had wanted all those years!*

The living situation was a bit uncomfortable, especially for Omaran, because the three of them had decided they weren't ready to tell Cathy's two sons yet, so Cathy and Mike were still sleeping in the same bedroom—though they were no longer physically intimate—and the new couple could only meet in secret. Omaran came over to the East Bay when he could, to meet with her in nearby parks, or sometimes they would just sit in his truck and talk. On the weekends, she sometimes went to his apartment for a visit when she could get away for a short while, or they took a hike.

The three of them got together once a week at Omaran's apartment. Keeping the energy as clear as possible between them was a high priority, so they meditated together, praying to be shown the highest path for all of them. They talked some about their feelings and possible futures, and the two men got to know each other better.

Despite the fact that Cathy was still living with her husband, Omaran did tell his parents and siblings about his new-found love, because they didn't live nearby. He also decided to introduce her to his three kids, without letting them in on her marital status. He was a bit uneasy about introducing her to them, due to the fact that he had hidden most of his spiritual life from his children because their mother did not share his interest. It had actually been a source of some discord in that marriage, and he had waited until they were finally separated before delving in full force. But by then, his children were almost grown and it seemed too late to share his experiences in depth with them.

Cathy, on the other hand, lived her spiritual life very openly, and had always discussed these concepts and ideas with her children, and with other family members while growing up. Omaran knew she really had no concept about how unusual this was, for she had always been around people like herself. He also knew his kids would probably be the most mainstream people she had ever been around, and they might not understand her way of looking at the world. They had probably never even met someone who had psychic abilities, or who could remember past lives and talked about them as if it were commonplace.

His oldest son had been living on his own for some time, but the two teenagers, a boy and a girl, lived part time with him in his apartment and part time with their mom. So Cathy saw the younger ones briefly when she visited, though they were very busy with their lives in high school. She sensed a deep love between Omaran and his kids, but also some deep pain. Her inner eyes could see a complicated web of energy cords between them, and some unfinished karma. Normally she would have been concerned by this . . . but she was blissfully in love.

Seven

I make love with you
with song and word,
I wrap you in a phrase,
one I've never heard.
I feel your gentle touch
upon my mind.
You are everywhere,
everything in time.

— From the song
"Perfect Harmony"

Since her angel-self had been awakened, Cathy was more determined to find her true name, the one that really resonated with her. Her childhood name had never suited her, and she had experimented with different versions of it, even asking her friends to call her by her middle name for a while, but never had been able to settle on one for long. She had often wondered why her parents had chosen for her a name she didn't like, and had finally decided that probably the quest for the right name was part of her chosen spiritual path. Since getting together with Omaran, it seemed even more important and urgent, like it had something to do with the spiritual work they would be doing together.

So one weekend she arranged to spend three days in the woods to ask for her name. She decided to join her sons and three of their friends, who were spending a week in the Ventana wilderness near Big Sur, a small town down the coast, to practice their survival skills. Backpacking over the very steep terrain, it was quite a trek to their camp. She pitched her bright blue tent a respectful distance from where the others had made their shelters out of available branches, twigs, and leaves. It had taken a bit of coercing for the boys to agree for her to bring a tent and some food for herself, when they allowed themselves little more than a knife. They had to catch or harvest everything they ate, which usually amounted to lots of herbs and small plants, a few berries and roots, and snakes, lizards, and bugs. It wasn't a diet Cathy relished, and honing her hunting and gathering skills wasn't what she was there for.

The first evening, they all sat around the fire at night discussing their adventures of the day. She listened to their stories quietly, laughing with them at their many mistakes as they learned the best ways to do such things as start the fire with a bow drill, or catch a lizard using a hooped blade of grass. She liked to see her kids in their element.

Her sons had never fit into normal society because they were different, like their mom, and they were very unhappy about the way modern societies were destroying the planet. They wanted no part of it. "Primitive" or "aboriginal" skills were their current passion, learning the older ways of living which were much more in tune with nature. Cathy was very glad that her appreciation of the sacredness of nature had stayed with the boys.

She had learned a lot from them over the last few years, since they had started studying history, anthropology, and environmental sciences, mostly from reading on their own. She had long thought that this was a slave society she was living in, with most people having to work incredibly long hours just to make a comfortable living, and a few people controlling most of the wealth. But it was surprising to learn that hunter-gatherers worked only about seventeen hours a week to provide for a whole family! That left much time for art, music, socializing, raising children, spiritual endeavors, and generally enjoying life. And this had been the norm for many thousands of years, until the agricultural revolution.

Cathy was proud of the way her sons did what they thought was right, despite the difficulties it brought them at times, because their viewpoints were so different from those of most people in western society.

The next morning, while the others were out gathering food and exploring, she sat by a small creek, leaning against a large redwood and cushioned underneath by a thick layer of mulch and moss. Breathing deeply of the forest air, and gathering the energy of the redwood trees to her like a magical cloak, she simply sat for a while, enjoying her surroundings and reveling in the beauty of creation, giving thanks for being a part of it. The forest was always her most cherished place to get inspiration and spiritual connection. Trees had such a wonderful grounding effect, their roots firmly embedded in the Earth, as well as acting like antennas, reaching toward the cosmos.

She contemplated her life. Here she was, starting yet a new phase. She had done many different things in this life, from being a jazz dancer, then a singer, to having a small business, to going back to school to become a geophysicist, all while raising her kids. Since her first major mystical vision as a small child, in which her spirit guides had reminded her about what she was here for and gave her basic information essential for this lifetime, she knew that she would be starting her most important work after she turned forty. That was why she had birthed her children when she was so young, so they would be grown by this time.

She mused about something her eldest son had told her recently. He remembered contacting her in spirit before he was conceived, and suggesting that she have a baby. He wanted her to be his mom, and he didn't want to wait until she was older to come in. So what if she was only eighteen?

"Don't you want to have a baby? Think about how cuddly they are, how much fun it would be . . ." He said he had been after her to make the baby body for him for months, before she finally decided to do it. At that time, she hadn't been aware that it was her future child prompting her. She only knew that she suddenly had a strong urge to become a mother, despite the apparent obstacles of being so young and still in college, not being married to the man she lived with, and having very little money. None of that had mattered to her at the time, and though it had been a difficult path, she was very glad that now her kids were grown, and she was still fairly young and very healthy.

She had turned forty last year. Her guides hadn't told her, in that first meeting as a child, what form her "most important" work would take, and she still didn't know. Did it involve Omaran? Was that why she hadn't met him until now? It would all unfold in time, she knew, and she could wait. This next phase of her life certainly seemed important, like all else was just preparation or last-minute housecleaning for her spirit.

Thinking more about Omaran, she realized that this was the first relationship she'd had in which there was no karma, no unfinished business between them. Their connection felt so pure, so clean. All the others before him had felt, even in the beginning of the relationships, like there were things to work out, parts that didn't quite fit that would have to be dealt with in some way. She had often thought that her relationship with Mike was like fitting square pegs into round holes, which had required work to smooth out over the years.

But with Omaran it was effortless. They fit together perfectly. Besides the fact that they were twin flames, which certainly must be a large factor in their connection, they had both deliberately worked on balancing their male and female sides, and perhaps that had something to do with it. It also seemed that their lives had been connected somehow even before they met. As they got to know each other better, they discovered more and more similarities between their paths.

Breathing in the smell of the redwoods again, she shifted into a more comfortable position, closed her eyes, and asked her Higher Presence for her spiritual name, so she could have the highest energy possible for the new journey she had embarked upon. Then she quieted her mind and listened.

"A."

One solitary letter, emblazed on her consciousness. She tried to be accepting, but thought it would be difficult to introduce herself. *"Hello, my name is A." "And how do you spell that?" "Just A." "Oh, and is that short for something?" "No, that's it. Just A."* She could imagine the looks she would get. She pushed aside her rational mind and continued listening. Hopefully there was more.

"AN."

Now they were getting somewhere. She listened some more and presently two more syllables came through.

"An-Te-Ra."

That was all. It sounded OK, and maybe it was even usable if she slurred it a bit rather than using its real pronunciation. But she was not sure whether she liked it or not. It would take some settling into. She thanked her Higher Presence and guides and meditated for a while longer before going back to camp.

"I got a name but I'm not sure that I like it yet," she told Omaran on the phone after arriving home the next day.

"Great! What is it?"

"I'm not going to tell you until I'm sure."

"What do you mean sure? If you got it in meditation, it has to be right."

"Well, we'll see."

"Yeah, it took me a while to accept mine, and you and Mike are the only ones who call me by it so far."

He really was anxious to call her by her spiritual name, since she was calling him by his, and intuitively he knew that she needed a name that matched his in vibration. But there was no reason to push. Their lives were already changing incredibly fast since they had met, so why try to speed things up even more?

It was a week later that they talked about it again, when they had arranged to do a channeling session over the phone. Sitting on her living room sofa, Cathy stretched the telephone cord as far as it would reach from the dining room. Omaran sat in his favorite chair in his apartment across the bay. They both put their phones on speaker and sat quietly. The Council of Seven gave them advice on their situation, and general encouragement. Omaran asked a few personal questions and got wise, loving answers.

As they were closing, the Council said, "And Omaran, we just want you to know that we call this being Antera in the inner planes, and unless she comes up with some other name she likes better, we will continue to call her that."

"Antera? I like it! Thank you for telling me."

"Indeed. We could see her reluctance, and decided to tell you. Now you can help her decide."

"Thank you very much for all your help."

"We leave you with our blessing and love."

Omaran was excited. Now he knew her name, and would start calling her that at last! Antera came back fully into the room and took the phone off speaker, relaxing on the couch to talk.

"How do you like that, Antera? I'm going to call you that from now on. I had a feeling it started with an A. I guess they couldn't wait for you to tell me."

"Hmmm . . . well, I haven't come up with any other name I like better."

"It's a great name! And now we are 'A and O,' like alpha and omega!"

In early April, only a few weeks after Cathy/Antera had made her fateful announcement to Mike, he was offered some geological field work down in Big Sur, through his job at a consulting firm. It would require spending quite a bit of time away from home. He had always before opted not to take projects that required travel, because of his family, but now he welcomed this opportunity. Field work was very enjoyable to him, and it really was the reason he had gotten into geology in the first place, not to sit behind a desk writing reports. He realized that this new freedom to travel would be one advantage of their separation. It would also be a relief to get away from it all, and he knew Antera would appreciate some time away from him . . . it had been so intense lately.

So it was that on Easter weekend, when Mike was away in Big Sur working and the boys were out of town on another primitive skills camping trip, Antera and Omaran slipped away and drove north to Mt. Shasta for a couple of nights. It was their first trip together.

In one of his "knowings," Omaran intuitively got that they needed to go up to the mystical mountain. He had been there and climbed to the top twice before, but felt there was more to the mountain than he had realized from those physically demanding trips. Antera had driven by on the highway, but had never stopped, though she had been excited by the sight of it—a lone, snow-covered peak rising far above the valley in such splendor. It could be seen for hundreds of miles on a clear day. The scientist part of her was fascinated by the fact that it was a volcano that hadn't erupted for hundreds of years. And her mystical side had heard that it was a powerful spiritual vortex.

It was too early in the spring to camp, so they had reserved a motel room. As soon as they got there in the early afternoon, they put on their warmest clothes, drove up the mountain and parked the truck. After a half-mile hike in the snow to Sand Flat, they stopped at a nice spot on the slope above the large, flat area and spread a wool blanket to sit.

They stared up at the mountain peak across the valley, framed by pines and firs. It was covered with snow except for a few ridges of jagged rocks. The mere sight of it seemed to transfix them both, and take them to higher realms of consciousness. Time went by quickly, and sitting mostly in silence together on the mountain while looking at the peak was surprisingly satisfying. So that is what they did, all afternoon.

"It is so wonderful here, I'm really glad we came," Omaran commented at one point.

"Me too. The presence of the masters, and the Christ Light is so strong, I feel like I could just sit here for days basking in it and not get bored."

"Yes, there seems to be a lot going on at a deep spiritual level here. I kind-of wish I was conscious of all that was happening," he said. "When I close my eyes, I feel energy swirling all around, but I don't know exactly what is going on. It feels good, though, like I am being cleansed in some way, prepared for what is coming next in my life."

Antera nodded and added in a hushed tone, "It really is a magical place."

He blinked, then turned to her. "You know what? I just got a message to build an etheric temple here that I can come back to in meditation, after I go back home."

"You mean just create it in your imagination?" she asked.

"Yes, then I can gather these energies any time I want, just by coming to my temple."

"What a good idea. I'll make one for me, too." She closed her eyes for a moment, picturing it. "Mine will be round, with a domed roof. I'm going to put it right over there where the fir trees are making a small circle."

"Mine will be next to that large pine, across on the other side of the valley . . . an octagonal shape, but with walls and a roof I can make either opaque for privacy, or clear, so I can view the mountain and stars."

They worked on constructing their temples in their minds, with complete details, and imagined sitting inside them for a while. Then, gazing at the peak again, they sat in silence until it became too cold for comfort, and Omaran revealed a plan he had been thinking about for days.

"I want to have a ceremony declaring our love and devotion to each other, like a marriage in spirit. Right here and now, where the presence of the masters is so strong." He was beaming. He loved to give her little surprises like this.

She was touched, and smiled. "All right, what do you want to do?"

He had been secretly practicing some lines in his mind, but wanted it to be somewhat spontaneous. "Stand facing each other like this, and call in our guides and the masters we want to be witnesses, then declare our love and make a spiritual commitment, with whatever we want to say."

"You lead, since it is your idea."

They stood and invited all the angels and beings of Light they could think of, and proclaimed their love and devotion to each other out loud before all their witnesses, whose presence they could feel all around them.

"We declare, before all the masters and the spirit of the mountain, and true to our Divine Presences, that we love each other with the purest Divine Love, that we are one in body, mind and spirit. We announce this spiritual marriage of twin flames at this time, in this place, and ask for your blessings, love and guidance!"

As they stood there, the energy poured into their souls, minds, and bodies, and they opened up further to their destiny—the destiny of twin flames, the merging of souls in the highest possible way while being embodied, the beginning of their spiritual service together. They had come together at last, against the odds but with tremendous help from Spirit. They both felt that it was meant to be.

The merging continued from spirit into matter when they got back to the motel and made love. It was the first time they could leisurely enjoy each other's bodies, the first time they had really been alone and unrushed, in a comfortable setting. It was an intense culmination of energies, a bonding at many levels, and a relief of tension that had built up for months. It was the beginning of a life of bliss between twin souls—or so they thought.

Eight

And as we reach out for the One
we feel the Light of the Golden Sun.
And when I open up my eyes and see
I realize all is me.

— From the song "The Light"

"I had a dream last night I want to tell you about." Antera paid attention to her dreams, or what she called "nighttime experiences," because often they carried meaning for herself or others, or warned her about things to come.

"What was it?" Omaran asked as he sipped his herb tea. They had met at the Depot for a late breakfast, a café at the center of Mill Valley in Marin, and were sitting at a small table outside in the sunshine. The fog that often came over Mt. Tamalpais from the sea had burned off to reveal a fine spring day.

"We were in bed together, when suddenly I realized there was someone else in bed with us. It was another woman between us."

That got his interest. "What did she look like?"

"I didn't see her clearly, but she had dark hair and skin. I asked you who she was, and you told me, 'Someone I have to say good bye to before you and I can really be together.' I said, 'I hope you will take care of it quickly!' Then I woke up." She looked at him to study his reaction.

"Wow." He pondered the meaning of it for a moment. "It has to be my ex-wife, but I thought I already cut all ties to her. Maybe more energy work is needed."

He genuinely wanted to be done with all the women in his past, so he pondered what he could do to further cut ties.

"So then how will you handle it?" Antera wanted to know. The dream had been a bit unsettling, more so after seeing his reaction, which told her he knew he was not finished with his previous relationships. It was not a good thing.

"Hmm . . . maybe I'll go up on Mt. Tam and do a ceremony of some kind to shift the energy. I have done a lot of healing up there. Yes, that is what I'll do."

She nodded slowly, thinking that it probably would take more than a ceremony to cut ties, but said no more about it.

A few days later, he went up to one of his favorite places, the God Talking Rock, which he had often visited while he was in need of healing. When he stood on the large boulder, he could see the ocean far below, a grand vista that always gave him perspective.

He arrived there not knowing exactly what he would do, so he sat quietly on the rock, watching the leaves on the bay and oak trees rustle as the cool ocean breeze swirled around the cliffs in unpredictable gusts. He thought about the important women who had been in his life. Then, quieting his mind, he closed his eyes and opened to receive insight. Not surprisingly, his mother came to mind as one of the primary relationships that needed healing. She had gotten sick when he was a child, and he realized he still had a lot of anger toward her.

He suddenly remembered when it had all started. He was seven years old, when the twins, his younger brother and sister, were babies. They seemed to cry most of the time, taking turns so that when one finally fell asleep, the other one would wake up and start crying. It proved to be too much for their mom, who one day had what they later called a nervous breakdown, sitting down and crying as much as the babies, helpless and unable to care for them anymore.

Frightened to see their mom this way, he and his brother were sent to their room and stayed there, listening to their mom and the babies wailing and their dad desperately calling relatives, trying to find someone who could come over and help.

After that incident, his mom had never been completely well again. They found out later that she was manic-depressive, and had a chemical imbalance apparently triggered by this incident. During her manic times she was energetic and seemingly happy, and acted like she was on top of the world, able to do anything. But when she was depressed, she was unable to do even the simplest tasks, or to make daily decisions such as what to make for dinner.

Unpleasant scenes from his childhood flashed through his mind. When she was depressed it was like not having a mom at all. Even though his dad did his best to compensate by giving the kids more attention, there was only so much he could do. Omaran felt the pain of abandonment, and the anger as if it had just happened. It had been so unfair. But at the same time, he knew that she hadn't done it on purpose, and he felt guilty for being so angry with her.

Omaran stood up and took a few deep breaths, imagining that he was letting the pain in those memories go as he exhaled. He wanted to be done with all the negative effects of his childhood, and this was a primary one. He again asked for help in releasing his anger, reaching his arms out and up, to God and his spirit guides for support. Suddenly, there was a distinct shift in his energy, as if the tone around him, if he could hear it with his physical ears, had gone to a more pleasant pitch or harmony. He knew he had been heard.

Sitting down, he opened to listen again. This time his ex-wife came to mind. The last few years of their marriage had been filled with strife, causing it to end poorly, and leaving emotional scars. Yes, he was still quite angry at her, too.

Standing up again, and taking a position of power with legs spread and arms reaching up, he declared aloud, "Please give me help in releasing both of these women from my energy field! I WANT TO FORGIVE THEM ONCE AND FOR ALL!"

He remained standing, lowering his arms, and waited for guidance with his eyes closed. The wind gusted against his cheeks, playfully flapping his sweatshirt and making him sway a bit, but he stood firm and unmoving as he waited. Presently, he heard some noises, and when he opened his eyes he saw two ravens nearby, digging in the dirt with their beaks. He had never seen ravens do that, and so close. He thought it must be a sign. "Ah! So I am to dig a hole and bury all this old energy?" There was a loud squawk from one of the big black birds, which he took as an affirmative.

Omaran climbed down from the rock and looked around for something to dig with, and a place soft enough to dig in. He settled for a broken branch, and dug a shallow hole at the base of the boulder, while the ravens watched, without moving away. When the hole was sufficiently big, he closed his eyes and gathered all the anger and pain he felt toward his mom and ex-wife, and with one big breath, exhaled and yelled it into the hole, until he felt empty.

He did that several times, saying good bye to them, then heard some loud squawks and noticed that the ravens had taken off in flight, the two of them flying around each other in circles, playing as they went higher and higher. They squawked some more, then disappeared into the trees.

He surmised that he was finished, and saw the ravens as symbols of him and Antera, who were now free of the old energy, free to soar together to greater heights from now on. He was touched, and felt gratitude for the mountain's help. "Thank you! Mother Earth, please take and transform this energy into Light. Thank you!"

The same branch served him to fill the hole in again and pat it down so it looked as if he had never been there. He hoped that now he was free of his past forever, and ready to move ahead with his twin soul to his spiritual freedom.

In late April, Mike, Antera and Omaran, after a lengthy discussion, decided that they had put off telling Antera's sons about Omaran long enough. The time had come. Mike's idea was to initially have Omaran over for dinner, as a friend of both of theirs, to break the boys in slowly. This turned out to be a pleasant encounter, with neither of the boys openly suspecting anything unusual. They enjoyed his company, and though he was nervous at first, Omaran was glad to finally meet and get to know his future stepsons.

The serious talk was instigated a couple of weeks later, when the family of four sat down for a meeting in the living room after dinner one night. Both sons sensed that something important was brewing, and had been going on for a few weeks, but they didn't know what.

Mike began, "We have something important to tell you, and it may be kind-of shocking." He gestured toward Antera to continue.

"Well, you remember Omaran?" she said. They both nodded. "He is my soulmate, and I am in love with him. We want to be together." She paused, to let it soak in. Neither son said anything. They just looked at her.

She continued, "So some things are going to change around here. I'm really sorry, the last thing I want to do is put you two through another divorce, but the pull between us is so strong I can't ignore it or resist it any longer."

They nodded, still too stunned to say anything.

Mike assured them, "Now, our situation won't change too fast. I really like Omaran and we will be good friends. Your mom and I are also going to continue our friendship, so I will be around. You aren't going to lose me, I'll still be in the picture. Anyway, it will take months to sort everything out, so I am not looking for another place yet."

She added, "The three of us are very determined to make this transition as easy as possible. We are getting a lot of help from our spirit guides."

They talked for a bit longer and the boys seemed to take it well, at least on the surface, then they went to their rooms to do homework. More talk would come later, but it was a relief to finally have the truth out. Another hurdle was cleared.

Since the boys knew what was going on, it was finally acceptable for Antera to begin sleeping in the living room, formally separating her and Mike, to everyone's relief. Mike wasn't in any hurry to move out, especially since his guidance continued to tell him that the time wasn't yet right. And though Antera wanted to have space to herself and more time to be with Omaran, she knew that it would be difficult to afford the rent on the house by herself, and also that it would take a while to sort through their possessions. So this arrangement worked for the time being. Neither she nor Mike told their relatives or friends what was really happening yet, because they agreed it was just too strange a situation for others to understand.

The three of them continued meditating together regularly, now able to do it in Antera's and Mike's home. Sometimes they would do a particular lightwork exercise together, such as connecting their hearts or building qualities like faith and courage, and other times they simply sat together in silence. The presence of their Divine Selves and their guides was very strong, soothing their energy fields.

On one of these evenings together, the three of them were sitting together in the living room and Antera got a message that an individual member of the Council of Seven named Zolta wanted to talk to all three of them. Until recently, she had kept her channeling mostly to herself, only occasionally doing a reading for Omaran, friends, or family members. This was the first time her guides had requested to speak to others "live."

She asked the two men if they wanted to hear what Zolta had to say, and they were delightedly receptive. It was a beautiful message about Divine love, and what the three of them were creating together. The energy that was transmitted to them during the channeling was even more profound than the words, and they were all transformed and deeply touched. It created an even stronger bond between them, weaving their energies together as one radiant beam of Light.

After that experience, Antera channeled for the three of them almost every time they got together, besides what was coming through for herself and Omaran alone. They were given very helpful advice about their changing situation, support for the process, and encouragement to continue on. Their faith deepened, hope brightened, and spirits soared by talking with these masters together.

These sessions were so powerful that the three of them decided to start sharing them with others, in a weekly guided meditation every Wednesday evening. Omaran started telling others about it, and the group gradually grew by word of mouth, as people brought their friends over. Zolta and the Council of Seven wove a beautiful tapestry of words, projecting the finest energies of Divine love as they gave their spiritual lessons. They spoke on many different subjects, sometimes answering individuals' unvoiced questions. In the process, everyone who was exposed to their loving energies felt like they had been transformed into a higher level of existence, as if they were bonded with their soul and could see the world through that wise perspective where the complicated dramas in their lives became clear and simple. Their hearts were opened to a new level each time, as their frequency of vibration was gently raised.

As more people joined these sessions, the evenings became more structured, with Omaran leading an introduction before Antera started channeling, and then encouraging people to share their experiences afterward. It was the beginning of the twin flames' spiritual service together.

Nine

She went soaring,
far beyond
human confines.
Soaring, upon
her wings Divine.

> — From the song
> "Beautiful Heather Blue"

Mike spent several days a week at his field job down in Big Sur, and before long met a wonderful lady named Patti who lived there. She was a few years older than him, with lovely, pure white hair and a beautiful complexion. Her deep blue eyes often gazed at him with adoration, and he soaked it up like a sponge. She was very smitten with him. They spent many hours together at the beach, talking and watching the waves crash through a large, rectangular hole in the rocks that looked like a doorway. It became their special spot. They found that they had many things in common, and spent a lot of time laughing. He loved her laugh, and she loved his jokes.

They saw each other whenever he was in Big Sur, and after a few weeks, he brought her home one weekend to meet Antera and Omaran. He really wanted to see what they thought of his new girlfriend. After hearing so much about Mike's wife and her boyfriend, Patti was a bit nervous about meeting them, but she was willing to be open to the creative arrangement.

Antera and Omaran were very glad that Mike had found someone to love; in fact they were relieved. He had been through so much, and it eased some of the responsibility and guilt that Antera was still feeling about the suffering she had put him through. Patti gave him joy, and after a brief initial awkwardness they all felt about being openly affectionate to their respective partners, they all got along fine. The four of them talked easily, and while they were sitting quietly together after a meditation on Saturday night, Mike made an announcement.

"I want to be called Michael from now on, not Mike. That is what Patti calls me, and it feels right for me now." He gazed lovingly at Patti, remembering the sweet way she addressed him.

Antera asked, "So do you think Michael is your spiritual name, then?"

"Perhaps," Michael replied, "I just know that I am a new man after all the changes I have gone through over the last few months, and the name change, however minor it seems, signifies my new persona. Plus," he added, "I have a strong connection with Archangel Michael and like the fact that I am named after him."

"Sounds right," Omaran confirmed, nodding approvingly.

"OK, we'll call you that from now on," Antera said.

Little did any of them know that Michael's big changes were not over yet.

Because it seemed that Mike/Michael would be moving out soon, in late May Antera finally told her parents and relatives about her change of mates. She couldn't keep it from them anymore, even though everyone in her family lived far apart, and now that it was well under way there was no need to. Her family of origin was a group of very old, dear souls, the parents and six kids all highly intuitive, who had incarnated together many times in different ways. It had been a very good upbringing, from a mom who was an artist and into "positive thinking," and a dad who was a psychologist, both of them having taken their roles as parents of a large family very seriously.

Antera was very glad to have been a part of such a group during her formative years, and appreciated it more as she got older, especially as she learned about what other people had gone through in childhood. She knew her folks would accept her changes with understanding as they always did, but that it would still be shocking.

"Mom, I have some rather shocking news." She heard the intake of breath on the other end of the phone line, and added quickly, "Don't worry, it's nothing bad."

"OK, what? I had a feeling something was going on with you."

Her mom had always been intuitively connected with her children, and it was hard to hide anything from her for long. But she always respected her children's privacy and waited until they told her. "Michael and I are getting divorced because I finally met my soulmate."

"Oh, my."

"His name is Omaran, and Michael likes him a lot. They are going to be good friends. It is all working out very well, and we are getting a lot of help from Spirit."

"Well, tell me about him."

"He lives across the bay, and he is absolutely perfect for me. A herd of wild horses couldn't keep me away from him. We amplify each other's Light, enjoy being with each other, and get along better than I thought possible with anyone. Much better than Michael and I ever did. You'll love him, he has such a good heart."

"I'm sure if you love him that much, we will too. Do the boys know?"

"Yes, we told them and they are taking it very well. Michael is still around and will be in their lives, so they won't be losing him, which makes it easier. He will be finding a place of his own in a couple of months, close enough to visit regularly. He already has a new girlfriend."

"Well, you sure know how to keep things interesting! I'll tell your Dad, better me breaking it to him than you, I think."

Antera was sure that was true. He dad, the grounding force in the family, was much slower to accept change than the rest of them. But he always came around in time, and as he got older Antera had noticed that he became more and more tolerant, though he was still known as the skeptic that kept them all on their toes.

She said, "OK, thanks. We are planning a trip down there in the next month or so, and you will meet him. Probably in July." They chatted some more before hanging up.

She called some of the others in her family and sent out a letter to the group explaining further what was going on. In early July, Antera and Omaran did fly to San Diego for a two-day visit with her folks. Just before they went, Michael sent a letter of introduction to Antera's parents, letting them know he was fine and that he liked Omaran a lot. Michael loved Antera's family and didn't want to break ties with them.

Omaran was just a bit nervous about meeting her folks, and wasn't sure he could live up to all the nice things Antera, and now Michael, of all people, had said about him. He had heard a lot about her parents as well, and really wanted to impress them favorably.

Upon meeting, Omaran was struck by the gentleness of both of them as they greeted him warmly. He immediately felt at home as if these were souls he had known for a long time, intuitively feeling that this was a family he had a long history with on the planet, old souls like himself.

Now I know what I missed out on in childhood, he found himself thinking as the four of them talked, sitting in the living room. The sun was relentless outside in this desert town, but inside it was pleasantly cool, due to a swamp cooler in the window. The older couple had their cooling system down to a science after living in the same house for almost 30 years, opening and closing windows at precise temperatures, measured by the many thermometers inside and outside.

Gaining greater understanding of Antera's upbringing by the minute, Omaran knew that he had, since birth, wished for a family who was spiritually aligned with him. He loved all his family dearly, it wasn't that, but he had always felt slightly different, like he didn't "belong" to them in a deep sense. He had yearned for his true spiritual family for as long as he could remember in this lifetime. Now, seeing what is was like for Antera growing up in a whole family of old souls, he knew just what he had been missing.

They spent the night, through the clamor of what seemed like hundreds of clocks chiming and cuckooing every fifteen minutes. Omaran found himself counting the chimes and gongs, relieved when midnight passed and they went back to single-digit numbers. He casually mentioned the unusual sounds in the morning, and Antera's dad laughed. He loved those old clocks.

"I hope they didn't keep you awake. I guess I should have turned them off, but we are so used to them that we just don't even hear them anymore."

"No, no, it was fine, I sleep like a log," Omaran said. "I'm just amazed to hear so many chimes."

"Only six, really."

"Well it sounded like a lot more," Omaran laughed, looking around the room and counting. He hadn't noticed them so much during the previous day, when other things were distracting him. There was a cuckoo clock from Germany with a bird that popped in and out, one that sang different recorded bird songs, a chiming mantle clock, and several pendulum-types.

Antera said, "I rarely hear them when I'm here, maybe because I grew up with them. They go right into the background. Kind of comforting, in a way."

"We don't forget what time it is around here," her mom noted, with a smile.

They spent the morning chatting around the kitchen table, then took a walk before it got too hot. Before leaving that afternoon, Antera's mom sat with Omaran and her for a meditation, and Antera channeled some messages for her. The experience was spiritually bonding and reinforced Omaran's feelings of connection at the level of spirit.

And thus, after over six months of secrecy, everything was finally out in the open and the new couple felt the relief of yet another hurdle jumped in their coming together.

Shortly after Antera and Omaran got back, Michael decided to move in with Patti in Big Sur. For reasons that Michael didn't fully understand, Patti was expressing a real urgency for him to come down to be with her, so he made arrangements at work and started packing. He reasoned that she must not be comfortable with him still living in the same house as Antera, which was perfectly understandable, and he knew it was time for him to move out anyway. Antera and he had already split their assets and debts in the fairest way they could, and the divorce was well under way.

Moving out was a process that took many weeks, because he was moving into Patti's small cottage in the redwoods, which was already fully furnished. He arranged to leave some of his things stored at Antera's house, especially household items he wouldn't be needing, for the time being.

After sleeping on the floor of the living room for the last few months, Antera was happy to have the bedroom again. Now Omaran could spend the night with her in comfort. Finally, it would be a semi-normal household, and she could start building her life anew!

But only two weeks after Michael had taken the last of his belongings, he called Antera with shocking news.

"Patti's dead."

"What? What do you mean?" It didn't quite register.

"I mean she's dead. Dead, dead. She drowned in the ocean."

She gasped. "Oh, my gosh! How did it happen? Were you there?"

"No, I was home with her son and his girlfriend, having breakfast. She said their visit had brought up a lot of emotional stuff to deal with, so she wanted to get out of the house for a bit. She told me she was going out for a drive . . ." His voice broke, and he blew his nose. "I heard a siren but thought nothing of it . . . when she hadn't returned by 10:30, I decided to look for her, and drove to our favorite beach, where there is that big hole in the rock. Her car was there, and a fire truck. I asked the firefighters what the problem was, and they said someone had drowned. I had a bad feeling, and told them I may know her. I did. I identified the corpse."

"Oh, dear. Are you all right?"

"I think I'm still in shock. Everything seems pretty surreal right now."

"Was it an accident? Any witnesses?"

He shook his head, forgetting that he was on the phone and she couldn't see. "No one saw anything. A passer-by found her body. She didn't know how to swim, so she could have just gone out too far and been swept under. The currents are strong there. But everyone is just guessing. I don't know anything right now."

Michael was devastated. Antera didn't know what to say. It was unbelievable that he would have to suffer this tragic loss so soon, when

69

he had barely gotten over losing her. He had just moved in with Patti and now she was gone, just like that.

She asked, "What are you going to do?"

"First I have to deal with the cremation and all the relatives. She has a large family, you know."

"I'm really sorry. Please let us know if there is anything we can do to help."

For the next few weeks, Michael found himself immersed in a whole new world of Patti's grown children and other relatives and friends, some of whom he hadn't previously met. A few of them had a hard time recognizing his position in the family. There were many things to be settled, and he didn't know much about the history of her financial dealings and such.

He wanted to stay in the little cabin in the woods he had briefly shared with Patti, but the landlord of their house wouldn't let him take over the lease, and he was forced to move out. He had no place to go and needed to leave quickly, so Antera invited him to stay with her until he could find a place to live more permanently. When she told Omaran, he readily agreed, as it was the least they could do. This time, however, it was understood that Michael would sleep in the living room. Antera and Omaran went down to Big Sur with the truck and helped him move some of his things back.

The process of handling Patti's affairs took a lot more time and energy than Michael had thought it would, and he continued to make frequent trips down to Big Sur. On one trip, he visited a shop in town that was owned by a friend of Patti's, where Patti had placed an order for a large amethyst crystal earlier that month. When he went into the shop, he learned that the friend had canceled the order when she heard of Patti's death, but he asked her to reorder it for him to remember her by.

When it arrived, it was stunningly beautiful, eight inches tall, with facets that radiated a soft violet glow. It reminded him of Patti's energy, peaceful, healing and loving. It became known as "Patti's Crystal" and from then on was always present on the altar of group meditations.

In the fall, after a couple of months staying at Antera's, Michael found an apartment he liked in Berkeley, despite the very tight market for rentals. There were so many people who applied for the apartment that the owner had to find a unique way to choose. He asked each applicant to write their name on a piece of paper, put it into an envelope, and breathe into the envelope before sealing it. He then asked a mystic friend to dowse the envelopes for the best tenant, and Michael won.

Now that Michael was in his own place, he had more time alone to ponder what had happened to him this year. The grief and healing that his marriage breakup had caused him seemed so long ago . . . was it only seven months? He really wanted to make sense of the whole ordeal with Patti. It almost seemed as if she had known her time was limited, the way she had insisted he come to live with her as soon as possible. Was it her role to push him into moving out of Antera's house? Certainly he would have stayed longer if she hadn't come along. He had been waiting for a sign that he should move out, and when the opportunity with Patti had come along, his guidance had clearly said to go for it. But what was the higher purpose of losing her so soon? Had he done something wrong, was karma coming back at him? Maybe it meant he was supposed to remain single for a while. . . .

His guides continued to console him and he listened to them often. His connection with them grew stronger and they comforted him as he grieved. Since moving out, he had made regular visits with Antera and the boys, and this helped him cope as well. It was also especially reassuring to the two young men, easing the transition in their relationship with Michael from stepfather to "uncle." And he continued to be a big part of the weekly group meditations, with Patti's crystal.

Ten

Well, I used to think
all I had to do was find you,
heaven would arrive,
the sky would always be blue.
I wanted to believe those
books and fairy tales,
all those 'happily-ever-afters'
that never seemed to fail.

— From the song
"Happily Ever After"

"Isn't it wonderful how everything worked out so smoothly? This has been some year! Now we are finally living together, my divorce is final, and we can get married."

It was a Sunday afternoon at the end of December. Antera and Omaran were cuddled together on the couch in the living room, arms and legs entwined. It was so delicious to be touching each other, that they sat close whenever they could. This was the end of a very challenging year, starting with that fateful phone call from Omaran in January. Now they were finally living together. After putting most of his things in storage, he had moved in, but hoped they could move back across the bay to Marin County as soon as Antera's youngest son finished high school in June. Omaran didn't want to live in the East Bay for long.

But as soon as Antera had said that, she felt his energy field change. She shifted her position slightly so she could see him. She had seen this happen before when she had mentioned marriage. "What's wrong?"

"Nothing," he fibbed.

"Why do you say that, when I can see that something is bothering you?"

It irritated him that she could read him so well. "It's just that my divorce isn't final yet."

"What? Your marriage ended many years ago! What do you mean?"

"We just haven't gotten around to filing the final papers yet."

She felt like he had hit her in the stomach. He knew she had worked very hard to get her divorce as quickly as possible so they could be married, and never mentioned this important fact before. What was going on here? Untangling her limbs from his, she moved further away and faced him.

"Why not? When will it be done?"

"I think it will be final in about five months, but I'm not sure. My ex is taking care of it." He avoided looking at her.

"Why didn't you tell me this?"

"I don't know, I guess I just thought there was no hurry. And I didn't really think your divorce would move this fast."

"I don't believe that. You knew I was pushing hard to get my divorce done before the end of this year. What about your promise at the waterfall to marry me as soon as I was free?" That commitment had been the turning point in her decision to leave Mike for him.

He shrugged and evaded her questions. He didn't want to think about it, much less talk about it. Standing suddenly, he left the room, pretending that he had something important to do in the kitchen, and the conversation effectively ended.

Antera continued to sit where she was, and stared out the window. A soft rain was falling and she watched the glistening drops coalesce and meander down the windowpane, distorting her view of the puffball tree and other plants in the outside world. *My inner world is distorted now, too,* she thought.

Trying not to take it personally, but unsuccessfully, she wondered what was going on with Omaran. There was a very tangible resistance in him to marrying her. Had he lied to her about thinking they were twin flames? If he believed they were, how could he possibly have any doubts about being together? It didn't make sense, and she was hurt, especially since she had given up so much for this relationship, and now he was acting as if he didn't want to commit to her. Hoping he would talk about it later, she picked up a book to read.

Omaran was almost as surprised as Antera by his reactions. He filled the teakettle with water and set it on the stove, turning it on. Now that she was free and ready to marry, he was having serious doubts. He didn't really know what was wrong—he had been so sure earlier, but now that he was faced with actually getting married again, he was suddenly terrified. What if it turned out like the last one? That relationship had been so bad that it nearly destroyed him. Was this one really different? Yes, his rational mind insisted that this really was different. He knew he loved Antera more than anyone he had been with. So what was he afraid of?

As he got his mug ready and filled the tea strainer with his favorite orange-cinnamon tea, he thought more about soulmates. He had always thought that once he met the right woman, everything would be perfect and they would live happily ever after. She would totally understand, love, and accept him. He thought about the many times he had mentally called to her over the last few years, describing to the universe what qualities she should have, the most important of which was having a strong spiritual connection. The reason his past relationships hadn't worked was because the people he was with were not his soulmates, and the match wasn't right. He really believed that. They had never understood him, or he them, so often there was friction.

When he met Antera, at first it had seemed like a dream come true. She had all the qualities he had asked for, they were on the same spiritual path, had the same goals, and enjoyed each other's company so much. Their connection was very deep. But now, a year later, after the newness had worn off, he found himself falling into old patterns. What was confusing was that his old ways of relating from his past did not work in this relationship, because she didn't let him get away with anything! She always called him on things that he was used to getting away with. He just wasn't comfortable with that.

If she really was his soulmate, shouldn't they get along fine and none of this happen?

Maybe she isn't my soulmate after all, he thought, *and this whole adventure is one big cosmic joke! I know I love her deeply and passionately, so why am I so afraid? I just don't think I could make it through another divorce.*

The subject of marriage came up a few more times in the next couple of months, avoided as much as possible by Omaran, then less frequently as time went on and Antera had to gradually accept that he wouldn't talk about it. When he was not being fearful, he really wanted to be with her, but when marriage was mentioned, the fear arose and he acted distant. It was very painful and confusing for Antera. He was like two different people, and she never knew which one to expect.

She found herself making excuses to her parents and relatives as to why they were not marrying, because she couldn't bear to tell them that after all that had happened, leaving her marriage and disrupting her life and that of her kids, her true love didn't want to marry her. He was the only one she had ever really wanted to marry, and even though she had loved her previous husbands, she had never thought, when she married them, that they would stay together the rest of their lives.

As painful as the situation was, she didn't know what to do but to carry on with their life together, which was deeply satisfying in every other regard. They truly enjoyed each other's company, so if she didn't think about marriage, her life was joyful and she was happy to be with him. But soon she found out that this was only the first of problems to come.

Continuing their weekly public meditations was very satisfying, and the group grew larger as word spread. They met and became friends with many like-minded people who were on compatible spiritual paths. Members of the Council of Seven came through Antera for the group, providing transmissions of energy through their words, and visualizations that were so filled with love that major, positive transformations were quickly taking place in the lives of many people who attended. Loving to be around spiritual family, which he had always craved, Omaran especially looked forward to these evenings. And the people who attended really felt like spiritual brothers and sisters.

Antera had told him months ago that she thought they would be teaching together, but one night after a group meditation, when she seriously expressed the idea of teaching a workshop on channeling, he proclaimed that he wasn't ready.

"I still consider myself to be a student, not an expert. I'm not ready to teach anything," Omaran said. "Especially not channeling."

"But I really think it is important for people to get their own guidance directly, without asking people like me to give them advice. I don't want to teach it alone. Together we are far more powerful than either of us alone. You have charisma and enthusiasm that attracts people and makes them feel good, and that balances my knowledge and skill."

"Yeah, but you've been doing this your whole life, studying metaphysics and having all those mystical experiences, so of course you are ready to teach. But I still have a lot to learn. Especially since I don't really channel." He folded his arms over his chest.

Sitting up, she tried to encourage him. "But you DO channel. You lead very nice guided meditations for the groups before I channel each week. Don't you think your spirit guide is speaking through you then? And what about when you write songs? That is a form of channeling also."

He wasn't convinced. "That's not the same as bringing through information like you do. I have big doubts about my abilities. Anyway, the answer is no, so don't even try to convince me."

The idea of teaching a channeling class made Omaran very uncomfortable, as it brought up many fears and doubts about his abilities. He had taken a channeling class several years earlier and successfully brought through his spirit guide verbally, but didn't keep practicing after the class. Over the ensuing months he had developed some kind of mental block about it, he thought, and never made the effort required, despite his desire to have the skill.

That evening when Antera channeled for the two of them, the Council addressed the issue with him directly.

"Omaran," the Council said, "if you want to have a direct verbal contact with one of us, simply ask for it, from your heart. When you are truly ready, it will happen. The verbal contact is an easy way to speed your growth, but only if you are comfortable with it, only if your fears are dissipated. You have put up some barriers to this out of your fears. . . . Do you wish to say something?"

Omaran marveled that they seemed to know what he was thinking. "Well yes, thank you. I would like to be rid of these barriers, these fears. I want to confront all these fears now. I'm ready."

"Are you sure you are ready?"

He hesitated. "I think I am ready."

"This is a tall order. These fears go back a long time."

"Do you mean just this lifetime?" He had a feeling this went back further.

"No," the Council affirmed. "You have been around here a long time."

"In a past life, did I go so far away from my body that I was afraid I wasn't going to be able to come back? Is that was happened?"

"You had an experience in one life in particular, where you were doing some activities that took you places you did not wish to return to. It got out of control. You felt you lost control of your being, of your consciousness. This has put the brakes on your connections. You decided never to do that again. You let some beings take control of your body, beings who were not high beings—they were astral sorts. And they inflicted pain on others."

Feeling the hair rise on his arms, he blew out forcefully. "Whew. That sounds familiar."

The Council continued, "This was not a pleasant experience for you. But it can be released with forgiveness and understanding. When you let go of your pain from this, your fear will also vanish, and you will be able to see the difference between that situation and the current one."

"I see."

"As long as you are working with guides who are of a high caliber, beings of Light, there is no danger of that kind of thing happening. High beings simply do not try to control you in any way. This would be counter to their purpose of aiding your spiritual evolution."

"Thank you, thank you very much. I feel very blessed to have your help. And I will work on this," he resolved.

With this new knowledge and after more encouragement from Antera, two weeks later Omaran did finally agree to do the workshop. She planned and outlined the course and gave him his part. He was very nervous at first, but they carried it off and they successfully taught a small group of students to verbally connect with their guides. Michael sat in on the class to strengthen his connection and help some of the other students. To his surprise, Omaran really enjoyed the experience of teaching, and seeing how much the participants got out of the weekend, but at the same time, a part of him now felt somewhat like a fake, and this started slowly eating away at him.

"I want to teach another workshop this spring, in a couple of months," Antera announced after dinner one evening. She was very excited about it and had been waiting all day to tell him. The boys had gone to their rooms to do homework, so they settled in the living room with some tea. "This one will present some of the processes given to us by the Council over the last year. We have benefited so much from them, that the Council is ready to share them through this class. It will be called 'Becoming a Master'."

"I'm not a master yet, so I don't think I can teach a class called that!" His stomach suddenly hurt. This teaching was happening way too fast.

She felt a cloud descend over him. "We don't have to be masters to teach about becoming one. It is a process, not an end point. A true master never calls himself or herself a master. Anyway, the channeling class went very well, didn't you enjoy it?"

"I guess . . . well yes, I did enjoy it. I loved it. But I'm not ready to teach a master's class." His voice got an edge to it as fear rose. "I'm just not as perfect as you think I am and I may never be."

"What? I never said you were perfect. I'm not either. What does that have to do with it?"

"To teach a class called 'Becoming a Master' I think you ought to be a lot closer to being one than I feel I am. I just don't want to teach any more. I'm not ready, and that is that. Leave me alone." He picked up the newspaper and pretended to read, shutting her out.

"Can't we talk about this? What's the matter with you?"

His fear was getting the best of him. "With me? Nothing's the matter with me, what's the matter with you? I just don't think it is a good idea. Why do you always think there is something wrong with me?"

She was taken aback. The dark cloud around him was growing. What was this energy? "If you're upset, let's see if we can figure out why, so it can be healed."

"I told you I'm not upset! There's nothing to heal. You just think you know everything." It irritated him even more that she wanted him to tell her what was going on. She wanted to talk about and examine every little thing that came up. And she seemed to know how he was feeling more than he did, though he would never tell her that. It was scary that anyone could know his innermost feelings so well, even when he tried to hide them. Why did she want to dig into old stuff, always looking for some deeper cause?

"Your anger is just energy that needs expression. It's not you. Any time you are upset it is a chance to heal something. If you don't discover the cause, it will just keep coming up again and again." To her, the growth process included going into the past to clear up the root causes of emotional pain. She looked at upsets as opportunities to heal something. Since she had started healing her own emotional body some twenty years previous, she had come to welcome any time she got upset as a possibility of finding out something more about herself, and healing another layer.

"Well, I'm not angry, and I don't feel like talking about it, so leave me alone!" He threw the newspaper down, went into the kitchen, and started filling the dishwasher, hoping she would not follow. He knew he was being overly defensive, as if that would protect him somehow, and hated this part of himself. If only he could be less angry over little things! But he simply couldn't seem to control it.

Seeing the energy barrier go up, Antera knew there would be no more talking with him. She also knew this had nothing to do with the new class, but was, instead, some kind of deep fear in him. Maybe he really thought that spiritual growth could proceed while ignoring emotional pain.

A deep sigh escaped from her and she picked up one of her seismological journals, scanning the titles of the articles. There were a few that interested her, and she opened to one, but her thoughts went back to Omaran. This moodiness was getting more and more frequent, and he didn't seem to have the tools to heal himself. And he sure knew how to squelch her enthusiasm.

She thought about the joy they used to have together, months ago, before he started being so moody and easily upset. Now, several times a week their conversations ended this way. A dark cloud of energy seemed to appear and surround him when he was the slightest bit upset, and this made him more upset, almost as if that energy was feeding his pain, or making it worse somehow.

Yes, she longed for the romance and the mutual desire to do their spiritual service together, to make a difference in the world. Though she felt that he still had those same longings deep inside him, it was becoming more and more difficult to talk or relate at times, because he was increasingly irritated over little things. She hadn't known that he had all this unresolved pain. How could someone be so advanced spiritually and so immature emotionally? Maybe she should have guessed, when she had first heard about his previous unhappy marriage, the problems with his kids, and his unavailable mother in childhood.

After Omaran finished cleaning the kitchen, he sat at the dining room table with his briefcase. He took out his calculator, pen, and a pad of paper and started to make a list of lumber and other materials for the job he was starting the next day. It was hard to concentrate on work. It felt as if he were becoming trapped in a situation that was not comfortable, with all this pressure from Antera to teach. He actually loved teaching when he felt he was well prepared, such as when he coached soccer. After hundreds of hours learning the game with one of the best coaches in the Bay Area, and time spent with one of the best coaches in the country, he knew what he was doing. And it was very enjoyable, especially because it gave him a chance to teach more than just soccer to the players that he coached, he mused, such as helping his team learn visualization techniques and encouraging them to believe that there were no obstacles that they couldn't overcome. And yet, here he was faced with an obstacle, and he wasn't handling it in the best way. He wasn't doing what he taught his players.

Turning his mind back to the task in front of him, the list of materials he would need first thing in the morning, he made some more calculations. However, his mind kept returning to that tight feeling in his stomach that appeared every time he thought about teaching spiritual practice. Was it fear? He would love to feel good about teaching with Antera, but compared to her he still felt like he was a beginner. It didn't matter that by the time they had met, he'd been on his own conscious spiritual path for some twenty-five years, reading books, taking workshops, using many different disciplines. He had been meditating for a decade, and had done extensive training on developing his Light body.

But never along his path had he thought he would be teaching any of it. He was still learning all the time, he was comfortable being a student, and he thought he had a long way to go before being a master of the human arena. A class on mastery? He snorted. No way. He turned back to his work.

Antera didn't give up on the class, but didn't talk about it for the time being, either, hoping that her guidance might bring some clarity to both of them. The members of the Council were such good teachers, and though they had been mentors to her all her life, in the last year they had expanded their lessons to include what Omaran was going through, and repeated for him much of what they had already taught her.

In the next session, the Council spoke directly about the new course, explaining more which exercises they thought could be presented and saying how excited they were about the possibility of sharing these with other people. Omaran felt better after hearing about it from them, and listened to them in a way that he wouldn't listen to Antera. They had a way of uplifting him and bringing him back to present time.

The way they described the class, it didn't sound that hard, and their enthusiasm rubbed off on him. Maybe he could help teach the class after all. They would be sharing processes and tools that the two of them had already gone through, and which, no doubt, would be transformational for others as well. He decided he would do it.

For the next few weeks Omaran's mood swings continued to get worse, depending on what was going on around him. Many seemingly outside influences threw him into upsets. He lost a contract, and feared that he couldn't pay his bills. His problems with his children developed into some painful interactions. He had hidden his spiritual practice from them while they were growing up, because their mother didn't share his interest. But now that they were grown, he naturally wanted to share that part of his life and experience with them—especially since he had come together with Antera, and his spiritual experiences had become more powerful, and such an important part of his life. But they mistook his exuberance and thought he was trying to push his beliefs on them, not understanding how he could "suddenly" be so interested in such intangible things. They shunned him, and this brought up his fears of losing them, adding to his level of anxiety.

From one minute to the next, Antera never knew whether she would have a loving mate or a distant one. After several months of this, her patience was wearing thin. He tended to take whatever was bothering him out on her, and she was getting frustrated at his slow healing process. It was very difficult for her to understand why he would always deny being upset, or not want to talk about it, when it was not something that could be hidden from her. He knew she was empathic. How could it be healed if he wouldn't even tell her about it? This was not her idea of an intimate relationship. She knew the real issues weren't between her and him, but the real cause was so difficult to get at with him.

After a display of his now-typical crankiness one day, she said in exasperation, "Don't you know that you have to release emotions? Emotional energy has to flow. Trying to hold it in will only hurt you! And what's worse, you're shutting me out as if I were the one who caused your pain!"

He knew he was being irritable. "OK, OK, I'll deal with it. I'll meditate and ask the angels to take away the pain."

So that is the problem, she thought. *He thinks that if he just keeps praying for help, the angels can just reach in and take his pain away without his having to do anything!* She said, "That is a cop-out. If it were that easy, no one would be carrying pain, and look around you at everyone! I'm sorry, but I think the only way out is through it. That means you have to look at it and allow it expression. There has to be some kind of physical release to heal it. It's just energy that is stuck!"

But he didn't want to hear that, and fervently hoped that he could get through it without doing any hard work. Confronting it at all seemed much too daunting. Maybe if he asked enough, a miracle would occur, and he would be healed. He prayed and prayed for the pain to be taken away from him so he could be happy.

In the next session with the Council, he asked them about why he kept getting upset. "I keep being frustrated by the same things. I know I shouldn't be upset so much, and I don't want to be, but I can't seem to control it yet," he said. "Please help me with this."

They advised, "If you see the repeat of an upset, it is because you have not dealt with it yet, and it will come up as often as it can, until you DO deal with it. Look upon these situations that trouble you as your most precious opportunities to grow. These are the times when you can make the biggest shifts in your life, simply by remaining conscious and not letting your old patterns, your emotional reaction, take control—by recognizing when it is trying to take control, and deciding to open your heart instead. Every time you choose to open your heart at a time when it wants to close for protection, you make giant leaps in your growth. It is only a matter of remaining conscious in the present moment. Do you see?"

Omaran answered, "That makes good sense, and I know it is true, but it is so hard to do. It is easy to say, but I haven't been able to do it."

"We can only give you tools, you have to choose to use them. A lot of fear has been coming up for you, and it desperately needs to be released. Old pains and patterns must be released for you to continue with your spiritual work. It is part of your cleansing process, and you are being given many opportunities to use all the tools you now have."

A lump formed in his throat, and he was on the verge of tears. "Yes, I can see that. I feel bad that I'm not doing better with this."

"Please don't be hard on yourself, that does no good. Instead, acknowledge your efforts and the times when you ARE able to take the higher path. As you grow and bring in more Light, there will be places in your emotional, mental, and physical bodies that don't want to open to the Light, that have been closed off for centuries, maybe thousands of years. This is what is happening with you, what you are dealing with."

"So parts of me don't want the Light?" This seemed a bit unnerving.

They clarified, "You have been able to function fairly well despite these painful areas, because they have been compartmentalized and set aside in a corner. But it takes energy to maintain those little prisons. The only way you can truly get all your life force energy back is to let the Light shine into all of those corners, and release them, one at a time. They will resist it at first, but there is a release that will take place as you open them up and look at each one. Acknowledge what is there and love it, then release it. The energy you had stored there will then come back to you.

"This exposure of old, compartmentalized pain is why, as you evolve and bring more Light into your life, issues will come up that you did not even know you had. Ones you have not wanted to look at. These are the very issues that need to be looked at the most! The ones that you resist the most, those are the ones that need to be addressed!

"This may require you to change something you have believed in for a long time, because humans often build up whole belief systems around pain, just to avoid it. So if you find these kinds of things coming up in your life now, it is good. And if you recognize them as a chance to grow, therefore embracing and releasing them, then you will be much happier, much more in the present moment. Do you understand?"

"Yes, I think so," Omaran replied, having a difficult time finding his voice around the lump in his throat. "But when I get upset, it is very hard to think about anything, and I doubt that I will remember this at those moments." He accepted these concepts completely, in theory, but applying them practically in his life was another matter.

"Bringing love into every situation is THE lesson for humans," the Council continued patiently. "Every time you get upset, you have a choice at that moment. You can give in to the emotional difficulties, the old patterns, the old ways of dealing with issues. You can give in to the fears, the perceived threats, the actions that may hurt others or yourself, because it feels comfortable.

"Or, you may choose IN THAT INSTANT not to give in to that. You may choose to close your eyes instead and imagine that you are channeling love from the highest source, and that the angels around you are sending you love and your heart is opening. Then ask yourself,

'What is the higher path here? How can I treat this situation with unconditional love instead of falling into my old patterns?'

"A solution will come to you if you do this. Just imagine your heart opening and free-flowing, that's all you have to do. Every time you chose love over fear, your heart opens permanently just a little bit."

"Thank you, thank you," he said slowly as he imagined doing what they suggested. "I think I can do that, just stop and focus on my heart and bring love to a situation. Thank you."

Afterwards, he thought about what they had said, and tried for a few days, sometimes successfully, to practice what they had taught. However, changing decades of bad habits and behavioral patterns was not an easy task.

Omaran's upsets came to a head in March, when he erupted in rage. One evening they were sitting in the living room talking, and something triggered a violent reaction in him. He suddenly got very angry and vigorously attacked Antera with his words, as if she were threatening his life. It was almost as if she could see a dragon slayer appear where her mate had just been sitting and talking, rising up with sword in hand to do battle. He said some very hateful things, then stormed out of the house, leaving Antera shocked and deeply hurt. She had not been prepared in the least for the onslaught. This wasn't just moodiness, it was blatant rage, and she was at a loss to explain what had just happened, and why her true love would say such awful things to her. Feeling that it must finally be over between them, she sobbed for hours.

When Omaran calmed down, many hours later, he came home and tried to make up. He knew Antera was not happy with him, but he didn't really know why, only remembering that he had been very angry. She looked at him incredulously, still reeling from his cruel words.

"Why do you hate me?" she asked with tears in her eyes.

"I don't hate you! Where did you get that idea?"

"All those mean things you said—that you want to split up, that you're sorry we got together, and you don't believe we are soulmates, much less twin flames, that I am a terrible person and the cause of your anger. . . ."

He didn't remember much of what he had said in anger, but it didn't seem all that bad to him. He said, "OK, I'm sorry."

"You're sorry? For what? Telling me what you really think?"

"I said I was sorry, what more do you want? Don't make a big deal out of it." He found himself getting angry again, because she wouldn't let it go. He thought she was making a big deal out of nothing, just like other women in his past. Maybe all women were overly emotional. He drew away.

Antera couldn't let it go. She couldn't imagine why he would attack her like that without cause. Her heart had been open and trusting to him, and now it felt like her energy had been violated, stripped away in one blow. He acted like this was perfectly normal behavior, but to her it was far from the loving relationship she expected. How could he say such mean things and then act like he had said nothing?

It took several days to heal her wounds and build her power back up, during which she stayed away from him as much as possible, and they didn't talk. For the first time, she had serious doubts about the relationship. No wonder he didn't want to marry her—he hated her!

After three days, Omaran couldn't stand it anymore and came over unexpectedly and hugged her. "I don't want to go on this way. I'm really sorry I acted so crummy. I love you and don't want us to be separate."

Looking at him and feeling the sincerity of his words, she could not resist holding him. There was no denying that the love between them was genuine, that they were meant to be together.

"Well why did you say those horrible things?"

"What things?"

She moved away, thinking that he had better remember them. "Like you don't think we should be together, like what a terrible person I am, and all the other mean things."

He flushed a bit, not remembering anything but a blur of anger. "If I said that, I didn't mean it."

"Then why did you say it?"

"I was just angry, I don't know what came over me."

"Angry at what? There was nothing to be angry about! We were just talking. There was no argument between us."

"I don't remember, but something sure ticked me off. I don't want to argue now. I said I was sorry. Come on, you know I love you." He reached for her again, and she didn't resist. She had missed him.

"Well it better not happen again."

"I'll be good." They hugged, and the affection slowly returned. Her heart melted under his charm. But a small energy shield had gone up between them, a slight protective barrier that she erected without being fully conscious of it. The violation of her energy by someone she loved so deeply, and toward whom she had been so open and trusting, had caused some lasting damage. She knew she couldn't totally trust him again . . . unless perhaps in the future he earned it back.

Eleven

Dear Mother Earth,
you give us life,
you give us such an opportunity.
Nowhere else
in the universe
is the experience so wild and free.

— From the song
"Dear Mother Earth"

Somehow, Mt. Shasta continued to draw them, so on the full moon of Easter weekend in April the two of them went there for the weekend to celebrate the one-year anniversary of declaring their spiritual vows to each other. For months they had been leading full-moon ceremonies and meditations in their home, and they had to cancel this month's gathering to make the trip. However, the group of friends had decided to get together without them, so they had promised to send energy from the sacred mountain to each of the group members at a specified time.

Driving into the small alpine town on the flanks of the volcano, they could feel a shift in their consciousness even before getting out of the truck. It was a sense of expansion, or gates opening to allow spiritual energies in that were not available elsewhere.

As soon as they got settled in their motel room, just after dark, they drove up to Bunny Flat, which was as far up the mountain as the road was open. They trudged out into the snow, which was several feet deep. There was a knoll a short hike away, and it called them as the perfect place to do the meditation and energy work. But a short hike in snow with low-cut hiking boots, sinking in up to their calves or knees with each step was slow going, and very cold. They quickly realized that they had not come totally prepared for such cold, but they had promised the group, so on they went. Antera's toes ached and turned numb, and Omaran's fingers felt just as bad.

"Just a little further."

"OK, I'm fine." Antera assured him. Omaran was always encouraging, like a good coach would be, Antera mused as she thought about the soccer teams he had successfully coached. She liked his positive attitude at times like this.

They found the perfect spot, where they could see the moon as it was just coming over the mountain. It was a glorious sight, huge and bright, perhaps magnified by the high elevation and thin air. Mesmerized, they stared at it for a few moments before turning their attention back to the task at hand. Right before the trip, they had bought folding chairs that came apart and packed into small carrying cases. They brought these out to put them together. It was the first time they had actually tried to put them together, and it turned out to be almost an impossible task in the frigid temperatures and wind. Their fingers didn't work very well, and the moon's light wasn't quite enough to see all the parts clearly.

As they struggled, tension built because the time was fast approaching for their promised connection to the full-moon group— then the situation suddenly seemed very humorous. Antera started giggling, and Omaran joined in. They had a good laugh at the ridiculous situation they had gotten themselves into. Just why had they promised to do this? What had they been thinking? The laughter warmed them and released enough tension so they were finally able to get the chairs together and sit. The chairs sank deep into the snow so that after all of that effort, they were still sitting on the ground, which brought another wave of laughter.

"OK, now, let's get serious. It's time to start." Omaran stifled his grin and they got as comfortable as possible. They gave their most diligent effort to transmitting the energy of the mountain and the gorgeous full moon to the individuals back in the Bay Area. Omaran read the names aloud one at a time, squinting at the list in the dim moon light, and they shook their bodies occasionally to make sure circulation was still flowing into their extremities. Each person got slightly less time than the one before, as Omaran gradually but unconsciously sped up the process. But they did finish, and could feel that the energy had been received.

Without taking them apart, they grabbed the chairs and hiked back as quickly as they could, reusing the foot holes from their walk in, with plenty of light from the moon. Their motel room was deliciously warm when they got back.

They had taken with them various work items to catch up on during their stay. But the first time Antera channeled the next day, the Council of Seven said that they thought it was funny that the couple had brought work with them. They recommended a weekend of initiation and purification, not work.

So, without putting up any resistance, the work was put aside and the couple went to Stewart Mineral Springs, a local resort, to purify their bodies. After that, they visited the same spot on the mountain where they had gone on their first trip together a year ago, when they had declared their love and union and built their etheric temples. They had since gone to those temples often in their minds during meditation and used them as special places for healing and energy work.

So much had happened in one year, and as they sat in the snow, they reminisced about how things had turned out. The whole ordeal of coming together, from that first phone call to the announcement to Michael only a few weeks later, to Patti's death, and then living together at last, was truly remarkable. The energy of the mountain uplifted them, allowing a perspective they didn't normally have.

Back in their motel room that evening, the Council took them through layer after layer of Light, a purification at many levels, and initiated them by helping them each symbolically let go of some attitudes and baggage that were weighing them down, taking them to new levels of vibration. The meditations they were taken through were very intense processes, and stayed with them for a long time afterwards. The veils were so thin on this mountain, the energies so different than where they lived, that their spirits could really soar.

On Sunday afternoon, as they were driving around on the mountain, bouncing on the stiff springs of Tan Man, Omaran suddenly said he wished they could stay longer.

"Yeah, a couple of weeks here would be nice," Antera agreed, "but I don't see how, with our jobs."

"Maybe later in the summer."

"But we don't have the savings to pay the rent and other bills and not be working. Neither of us gets vacation pay."

"Well, maybe it will happen somehow."

Antera thought for a few minutes while she watched some small snowflakes drift down outside the truck window. Snow was a novelty to her, due to her southern California upbringing, and she loved to watch it, allowing it to momentarily distract her. As she tried to follow the paths of the flakes with her eyes, an idea presented itself.

She shared, "The only way would be if we gave up the house and put all our things in storage, so we didn't have to pay rent. Maybe we could do that between houses, like when we are ready to move to Marin."

Omaran jumped on it. "Yeah, maybe we could go right after high school graduation, and stay for a few weeks, camping on the mountain so our costs would be low," he said.

He couldn't wait to move back across the bay to where he had been living for eighteen years before moving in with Antera. Despite the fact that she didn't really want to live in Marin County because she thought the people who lived there were much less aware than the Berkeley area, plus the rents were quite a bit higher, Antera had agreed to go as soon as her youngest son graduated from high school in June.

"That would be really great. Do you think we could pull it off? Just put everything we own in storage and hope we can find a house when we get back?" She was getting excited. It was sounding more and more like an adventure, which they both thrived on.

"Hmm . . . come to think about it, I don't have to be back until my soccer coaching starts, in mid-August. Maybe we could be here for six weeks!"

"I don't think my boss will like it, but wow, what an idea. Let's do it!"

They started planning and it became more concrete. It was exciting. The high-school graduation was only two months away, and suddenly there was a lot to do. They were definitely caught in the grip of the mountain. . . .

When they got back home, they told Antera's sons about their new plans. Both thought it was a fun idea. The eldest was attending San Francisco State University and ready to get his own house in the city instead of commuting, and the youngest decided to come with them for the first couple of weeks, until his apartment was available where he was going away to college in the fall. Antera and Omaran had been a bit concerned that he would feel lost for the two weeks, with no real home but their tent, but he tended to look at life as an adventure, so it was something he really looked forward to. In fact, he said, "I'm proud of you. It is not something people usually do at your age."

Well, that was certainly true, as they found out when telling friends and relatives. Most couldn't believe they would do something so "irresponsible" and "impulsive." It was as if they were just leaving everything on the spur of the moment. Most middle-aged people planned things for a long time. And were they coming back in August without a home, and possibly without jobs? Some relatives expressed big concerns. But the angels who guided Antera and Omaran had warned them of this, and kept reassuring them that all would be well, so they continued with their plans, ignoring the fears of others.

The two months went by fast, and they really didn't have all that much time to think about what they were doing. Since Omaran was busy, his moodiness was kept to a minimum. Besides working full time and packing, they were teaching the Becoming a Master class, once a week for six weeks, with about twenty students. The changes and healing that people were going through as they were exposed to the transformational processes from the Council made it well worth the effort.

When the time came to be out of the house, they packed Tan Man with camping essentials and took off for the mountain, with anticipation of a new set of adventures. They did not know where they were headed except that it would be somewhere in the forest in the midst of the famous Mt. Shasta spiritual vortex.

Twelve

Thanks for the land we live on,
the waters too,
and all the beings who call you home.
Thanks for the beauty here,
the sweet air we breathe,
accept our love, you're not alone.

— From the song
"Dear Mother Earth"

"We are in paradise, aren't we?" Omaran commented lazily.

They were sitting on a large boulder by a beautiful little stream, its water bouncing merrily over the rocks. The warm air was filled with flower fragrance and moisture. The water was very cold, but they had found a small pool just big enough to dunk into fully, then get out as fast as possible. They had just "baptized" each other in the pool as a blessing on their new life together and their dedication to Spirit.

"This is the life." Antera leaned back on the big flat rock where they sat, letting the sun dry her body. No one else was around, so they had gone in the water nude. Her skin was tingling. "I hope we can find water to get in every day the rest of our time here. It is so refreshing."

They had been camping for three weeks, and had discovered a perfect campsite, very secluded within the fir trees but with a perfect view of the mountain. The city energy was just about drained from their systems, and they had adjusted to a slower pace. The days seemed many times longer than ever before, each one more like a week of their "normal" life.

They were starting to really know the mountain and surrounding areas. Their days consisted of meditating, reading, writing, and channeling, as well as hiking. They spent an amazing amount of time just staring at the mountain, which seemed to change daily. The infusion of energy from this place was touching each of them at a deep level. Antera's main challenges had been physical, with headaches for the first week while her body adjusted to the fine vibrations of the mountain, and Omaran's challenges were emotional. He was extremely touchy, but with all the meditation they were doing, his frequent difficulties didn't usually last long. They enjoyed each other's company thoroughly, finding it very complete to spend all their time together.

Already they had learned a lot from their spirit guides and the spirit of the mountain. They had gotten in touch with and released some great sadness, a sadness they both had carried for thousands of years for the destruction of Lemuria, a land they had loved and felt very close to. It was said that Mt. Shasta was somehow connected with that lost land, and it was no wonder they were so drawn here. Memories continued to surface for both of them of a time when they had been together in Lemuria, and had been trained in the temples as land healers. Working together, their job had been to sense any disturbances or inharmonious energies in the lands, caused mostly by people's thoughts and actions, and to project healing energies to those places. Those ancient skills and abilities were slowly reawakening in them by being in this place.

The sadness of those memories arose from seeing the ancient land become progressively out of harmony, especially because of a large influx of newer souls who had been born. Because they were young, inexperienced souls, this group had caused a lot of disturbance. They were not in synch with a way of life that had worked for the older souls for thousands of years.

As the land became troubled faster than Antera, Omaran, and the other land healers could soothe, the disharmony had manifested with natural disasters and weather changes—droughts in some areas and too much rain in others. Finally, it culminated in tragedy as the land broke up in huge upheavals. A sense of failure for not being able to mitigate the disaster had been carried by the couple ever since, and it was a time for self-forgiveness and a realization that they had done all they could in the face of the inevitable. They both had done some weeping upon uncovering this loss of the land of paradise.

"What do you say we go to the mineral springs Thursday? It would be a nice way to celebrate my birthday," said Omaran. They had been there in April on their last visit, and he loved the invigoration they felt after making several rounds of soaking in a warm bath of mineral water, sweating in the sauna, then dipping in the cold creek.

"Sounds great. How about celebrating right now?" She giggled as she crawled up on top of him, rubbing her body on his, and they playfully made love on the uncomfortable rocks. Afterwards, they dipped in the water again, then sat on the rocks to dry, in silence.

As Omaran dozed, Antera watched and listened to the water. Creeks had always been fascinating to her, partly because she had grown up in the San Diego desert where running water was only seen immediately after it rained, which was rare. She remembered running excitedly, with her brother, to the local creek bed after it rained to see if it was running.

She hadn't seen her first real river until she was ten, on a camping trip with her family. They had stopped at the Kern River in southern California, and she had sat on a rock staring at the huge amounts of water flowing past, so transfixed by it that she had suddenly fallen, with all her clothes on, into cold water deeper than she was tall. It was as if the river had hypnotized her, and to fully experience its essence, thought it necessary to pull her all the way in. Her dad had pulled her out and still occasionally liked to tease her by saying she had jumped into the first river she ever saw.

Watching this creek now, she thought the running water itself must be incredibly wise, having the voices of so many words, and yet no words—like the wisdom of the Earth was being told in song, and in beauty. If only she could tune into it and really hear and see, maybe she would decipher the language and learn what the creek had to tell. Each drop must be carrying the history of the planet with it, as it moves over, under and above the planet's surface, experiencing countless forms and places. She mentally asked the water for some of its wisdom, for whatever it could teach her.

Immediately the message came to her that the sound of the creek contained almost every frequency, close to white noise, each tone caused by the different sizes of rocks it was falling over. As she listened more carefully, some tones stood out for a while, then others. The creek was playing a song, varying its dominant tones ever so slightly, and it seemed to tell her to hum with the water's song.

So she started humming, following the lead of the creek, and became so tuned to the water, that she was sucked into another space, a subtle state of consciousness where she felt a complete oneness with the water and the place. The wisdom and ancient nature of the water became a part of her own experience, as she sensed the vast age of many of the drops, and their individuality—so many drops constantly going by on their journeys, interacting with whatever came their way. Even though each drop had its own separate path, and went by quickly, there was a tangible oneness they all shared in this place, at this time. And though the parts that made it up were constantly changing, the entire creek had a spirit and presence of its own.

The variety of tones she was humming also produced vibrations in parts of her physical body, especially in her throat energy center, which opened up beautifully to a new level. It was as if frequencies that were missing in her energy were filled in, becoming more balanced and whole.

Feeling totally blessed, after a period of time she couldn't have guessed at, she went back to where Omaran was napping and tried to share her experience with him, though words were inadequate to describe what she had just been through. Omaran listened to the creek and toned with it also, for a time, and had his own transcendental experience. They both felt so grateful for all the gifts and experiences they were being given. They leisurely put on their clothes and boots and hiked back to the truck through beautiful countryside, under the clear July sky.

That evening they sat by the campfire, as usual. Evenings at 6000 feet elevation were pleasantly cool, requiring jackets and hats, and every night they had a fire to warm them and a lantern for reading. They had set up quite a comfortable home in the woods. There was the kitchen area consisting of boxes of food, camp stove, and ice chest; their bedroom inside the large tent; and the campfire area. The folding canvas chairs were moved around to follow the shade during the day, and positioned by the fire at night. They had seen no other campers since being here, mainly because they had chosen a road mostly overgrown by manzanita bushes, and they had plowed through not caring if the truck got scratched. The bushes kept others from their special spot.

"How about Lilly's for dinner after the mineral springs on your birthday?" she asked. It was their favorite restaurant in town. Most of their eating was at camp, but Antera thought a birthday called for a special splurge. They had managed to spend very little money while living this way.

"That sounds perfect to me. We can wait until the kids get here to have a cake."

They had invited all of their kids to visit and celebrate his birthday, and they would be arriving the next weekend. Though the two sets of stepchildren didn't have much in common, it was good to get them together occasionally. Omaran's daughter had announced to him by phone that she wouldn't be joining them, telling him only that she had some resentment from childhood and didn't want to talk to him about it. This hurt him a great deal, but he decided to try and put it aside for the visit. At least all four of their sons would be there and he was happy about that.

"There's the moon!" Antera saw it first. They had been watching it every night, changing slowly in form, and there was something very magical about it in the forest. When it was full, the snow-covered peak could easily be seen, and it was so bright that shadows were cast by all the trees. They had also noticed that the coyotes howled more often, other animals made more noise, and they saw more animals on their hikes at the time of the full moon. During the new moon it was much quieter and animals seemed more secretive.

They stood up and put arms around each other while they watched it rise. Though it was a few days past the full moon, it still reflected considerable light. Omaran had never before paid so much attention to the lunar cycles, and it thrilled him to follow the moon's progress every night through its phases. Jupiter, Saturn, and Mars had also moved noticeably since they had been there. Seeing the sky so clearly made them feel more and more connected with the changes of the heavenly bodies and their dance around each other. It seemed to reach him and resonate at a deep level in his body. They drank in the beauty, giving thanks for being so blessed, then got ready for bed.

"I'm going to try and find out what animals are making all those sounds at night in our kitchen area," he announced. "You go ahead and get in the tent, and shut out the light as usual, while I hide out here to watch, OK? Maybe we can fool them." He had been thinking about this for days, and tonight was the night.

"OK." She giggled, very entertained by his attempts to talk to and understand the wild animals around camp. Last week, when they had discovered that some critters were chewing holes in the tent around the edges, he had started pausing before getting into the tent at night to emphatically state out loud to them that the tent was off limits, but they could chew anyplace else they wanted. It seemed to work, too, because the chewing on the tent had stopped after the first night of this. But they had found that something had chewed up the cloth of one of their chairs instead!

Lately, every night after they got into their tent, all was silent until they turned out the lantern, then the loud noises started. It literally sounded like large groups of animals were having a party out there in the kitchen area, scurrying about, chasing each other, eating who knew what, though their food stores seemed hardly touched. So this was the night he was going to fool them, to see just what was happening out there.

He pretended to get in the tent, and Antera turned off the lantern. Flashlight ready, he crept behind a tree in the dark, hoping to catch them in the act. He sat in total silence, as still as possible, for a whole hour, but alas, the animals weren't fooled. They didn't budge. How did they know he was there? He finally had to give up and go in, and as soon as he was in the tent and turned off the lamp again, the animals were immediately out in full force. Antera and Omaran burst out laughing. It was a lot of fun being together.

The next morning they did their usual formal greeting of the sun, had breakfast, meditated and read. In the afternoon, they went on a hike not far from their camp, to explore a canyon and see if it contained water further up. It was dry, but they enjoyed the hike anyway, as always. They stopped to sit on some large volcanic boulders. Tuning into the creek the day before had been so successful, that they decided to see if the rocks had anything to tell them. They listened, asking for whatever the rocks or nature spirits of the place wanted to share.

The rocks immediately became alive to Antera, as if they were sentient beings willing to communicate. As a scientist, she was well aware of the scientific definition of life, and rocks definitely did not fill those requirements. But at the same time, she could sense life-force energy pulsing through them just as it pulsed through plants, animals and people, so she had long ago decided that the scientific definition must be too limited. Certainly in other cultures, where people were more tuned to nature, people considered everything, including rocks, to be alive and full of spirit.

As she sat looking at the speckled gray-pink boulder beneath her, she could "see" the energy lines pulsing through it, little pathways in a complicated network of currents flowing throughout. Indeed, there was a lot of energy here—the minerals that made up the rock seemed to be communicating and exchanging energy with each other, as well as with her. The energy flow was slower here than the flow she had experienced at the creek, and much slower than between people, animals and plants. But otherwise, it was no different.

The rocks told her that they teach silence and patience, which seemed like obvious qualities of these "beings." As she listened further, they also said they were storehouses of Earth history and wisdom, to be imparted to anyone who was able to communicate directly with them, or indirectly by sitting on them for long periods of time. She also learned that it was very beneficial to human physical bodies to be in direct contact with rocks, because the minerals in bodies resonate with the minerals in the rocks, and this heals and purifies them. Plus, by touching rocks with hands and feet, bodies get magnetically recharged.

Omaran also enjoyed the rock meditation, and felt very connected with the rocks, sensing the energy as a very deep feeling of peace. As he sat on the boulder, he merged to become a part of it, almost as if he couldn't distinguish himself from the rock. As often happened when they sat together like this, however, he had fleeting thoughts of wishing he could receive messages from the other side as well as Antera could, and feeling like he wasn't getting as much out of these experiences as she was. He put those thoughts aside so he could concentrate on the experience at hand, and mentally reminded himself that he was fortunate to be with her and benefit from her experiences and channeling.

On their way back to camp they hiked a ways down the dry creek bed, and both of them could feel the flow of the stream that coursed down the gully when it rained. The "ghost flow" was so tangible that they imagined being that water as they walked downstream. Into pools and out, over or around rocks and branches, they tuned into the way it splashed downhill. They became more fluid, and instead of individual steps, their feet glided down, smoothly and lightly, going faster and faster until they were effortlessly running, their feet barely touching the ground. They hummed as they went, seeing themselves as part of the stream of water. It was so vivid and joyful that the hum became giggles and then laughter, sounds that seemed to perfectly match what they were feeling, blending with the echoes of water laughing as it flowed over the rocks in the same way.

Thirteen

As my Higher Self,
expanded out,
looking down upon the Earth,
I am feeling unlimited,
no doubts
thinking about my next birth . . .
I'm so strong, I'm so strong
bring it on, bring it all on!

— From the song
"Bring It All On"

On Omaran's birthday, they got in Tan Man and headed down the rocky road to town, then off to Stewart Mineral Springs. When they arrived, they each picked their own small room with a bathtub, and filled it with the special hot mineral water. They got in to soak, remembering not to rub their skin, though the inclination was strong because the water felt so slippery. Antera had made that mistake before and paid for it with a severe rash afterwards. Just soaking in the water drew out toxins and stale energy. They called to each other after their agreed-on fifteen minutes were up, got out of the tubs, and met in the sauna to sweat. All their pores were opened and the sweat came pouring out. When they had enough of the heat, they went outside to the very cold creek where there was a small pool and took turns dunking all the way in and back out as quickly as possible. It was quite exhilarating!

After they had made this round three times, they sat out on the deck in the late afternoon sun. All their senses were more alive. The large creek loudly rushing over giant boulders below them, and the wind swishing through the pines above, were delicious sounds to their ears. Rich smells of the forest permeated all their cells. Their skin felt as though it was absolutely buzzing with renewed life.

Omaran was feeling so good, that he suddenly stood up, spread his arms to the sky and said out loud, "OK, I'm ready! I'm really ready! I want to heal ALL of my emotional body RIGHT NOW! So hit me with it!"

He was beaming, radiant. Antera smiled and hoped that his Higher Self would know that he was not really ready for being hit with all of it at once! But the universe heard his sincere wish and did not let him down.

The next week was pure hell for both of them. The kids visited for a couple of days, and as soon as they were gone, he turned into a raving madman, angry at anything and everything. They couldn't talk about even the most benign subjects, without him acting like he wanted to seriously harm her, like she was his most deadly enemy. Though he had enough control not to harm her physically, vile words of hatred came out of his mouth. Antera tried to talk only when absolutely necessary, but still found herself drawn into conversations that would go nowhere because he turned almost everything into a one-sided battle.

She was living with a madman, literally! He would say over and over that he hated her and thought they should not be together, then the next hour he would be apologetic and say he didn't mean anything he said! She thought it was like he was being possessed, like demons were freely taking over his body and making him say those awful things. The dark cloud she had often seen come over him when he was angry was now bigger and more present than ever, feeding on his hatred. She truly didn't know what to do now. She had never encountered this kind of behavior, and her heart was being ripped to shreds by such verbal abuse.

Omaran, in his periods of sanity, didn't know what to do about this anger. The magnitude of it had taken him by surprise. What was wrong with him? When he had asked to clear all his emotional body right now, he had no idea this would be the result. What had he done? He mentally tried to take it back. *I didn't really mean it! I want to heal in small steps! This is too much. I'm not ready!*

Where was this incredible anger coming from, anyway? He thought about how, in the past, it had always been the little things that would draw unexplained bursts of anger from him, rather than the big things. But this was different than anything he had ever experienced. It didn't matter what Antera said, he would internally find fault with it even before she finished speaking.

He didn't like acting this way, unable to stop saying terrible things to the woman he loved. Deep inside, even as he was getting angry, he knew she was right, and he must find a way to deal with this. He remembered her words, that it was just stuck emotional energy that needed to be released—that it wasn't him. But those thoughts couldn't hold sway against the rising tide of anger that continued to overcome him. He felt like he was in a whirlpool, with no idea which way led out. Several times he thought, *I wish we had never come to this mountain!*

After three days of this, Antera started scheming about how she could leave him, but it was not an easy thing to do. Her car was down in the Bay Area, she didn't have much money, and she really had nowhere to go. There had to be a good reason for this setup, but she couldn't think of anything good coming of this. She had known he was moody, but this hatred was something else! Twin flame or not, she didn't want to take this kind of treatment from anyone.

She finally holed up in the tent to get direct guidance, asking Omaran to leave her alone for a few hours to meditate. But when she asked her guides about it, she wasn't happy with the answer they gave. They gently explained that it was part of her mission to help him heal.

"You agreed to try to help him, before incarnating this time. It was clear when you were arranging your current life plans that he had some major healing to do, from issues that go back far before this lifetime. And indeed, the original agreement you made goes way back to when the two of you first came to the planet, when you said that the stronger soul in the end would help the other one so you could leave the planet together, if possible. Twin souls ascending together is so powerful and so rare!"

"What? I don't remember making that agreement. Why would I have agreed to such an impossible job?"

They answered, "Because your love is so great. Only a love so strong can heal him, and you really can learn to stay centered and strong even in the midst of being attacked. We assure you, he will be worth it! And besides . . . if you can't help him, probably no one can."

She wasn't at all sure she could do it, and thought it might destroy her in the meantime. "Ha! My love isn't very great. Right now I don't feel very loving toward him at all. I just want to get away. I don't think I'm up to the task. I thought I'd learned to stay centered with my last husband, but this with Omaran is the ultimate test, and I think I've failed already!"

"You are stronger than you think."

"How can I do this?" she retorted. "Don't I have a choice here? I mean, what about free will? Can't I just decide to cancel the agreement and move on to other service?"

"Yes, you could do that. . . ."

"What would the consequences be if I left him now?"

"In his current state, that would be devastating to him, and set back his healing process for a long time. Only with your love can he come through this crisis now. Do you think there is anyone else on the planet who could love him more than his twin flame does, and who could have the patience and understanding that you have? All he needs is love, period. Just love. This is your challenge. We know it is asking a lot, but if you can master this, you really will be the embodiment of Divine love."

Despite her resistance, she could feel that what they were saying rang true deep within, and that she really did have a soul conviction to help him if she could. The agreement was strong. She relented into the decision of staying, at least for a while. "But if the task turns out to be just too difficult, I reserve the right to cancel the contract! Is that all right?"

"Of course. Please keep in mind that when he does come through his pain, he will be the perfect mate for you. He still has all those qualities you find so joyful, they are simply hidden beneath his pain now. He will need time. You will be glad you stuck it out, for your own benefit and evolution as well as his. Bless you, dear one."

Over the next few days, it did help Antera cope when she thought of her interactions with Omaran more like challenges, rather than thinking she was a victim. The masters seemed to think he was special. Getting together with him must have been a cosmic trick, she decided, because she would never have gotten involved with him if she had known how emotionally damaged he was. It was like a veil had gone over her eyes, to keep that from her in the beginning, and she had only seen the true spirit, not the baggage. And perhaps it came down to that old phrase, "Love is Blind."

His anger did start to subside after a week or so, which seemed like an eternity, and despite her efforts to remain detached, by then she felt very battered and wounded. The anger was still just under the surface, though, because he didn't have tools for releasing it and wasn't interested in what she suggested.

At least he would still listen to the Council. They soothed him with their words each time Antera channeled for him, and sometimes they helped him get in touch with some of the deep pain he was carrying from many lifetimes. Several times he cried and felt much better afterwards, as if a small weight had lifted. But it wasn't sobbing, only a few tears. Antera thought he would be fine if only he could let loose and let it out! Too much conditioning from childhood had made that avenue of release seemingly inaccessible. "Big boys don't cry."

It was such a slow process that Antera was at a loss as to how she was supposed to help him. All her guidance kept advising her to do was to love him—simple in concept, difficult in practice. So her challenge was to love him while she was being attacked? It seemed impossible. As much as she tried, his words still tended to hurt her. She knew she was taking on some of his pain, and was gradually feeling heavier and less loving toward him. Though she knew how to cry and did so often to release her own tension, resentment was slowly building up.

During the brief times when Omaran was lucid, he agreed that he wanted to heal, but for some reason he couldn't accept help from her. So she simply started to study his behavior, in hopes that she would understand it better. She was no stranger to anger and rage. She had felt it herself, back in her twenties. She thought back to her second marriage, and how her husband then had pushed her buttons so much by deceiving her, that she had experienced anger that was on the edge of being out of control, blinding anger that made her want to do serious bodily harm to him. He had a way of infuriating her so much that if she hadn't had such good control over her actions, she could have physically hurt him.

That had been a karmic marriage from the start, with as much hatred as love, loving each other deeply and passionately one minute and shouting hateful things at each other the next. When this rage had surfaced, she had realized that she needed help. It was a scary thing, and highly unacceptable to feel that kind of destructive energy welling up in her, no matter what her husband at that time had done.

So she had begun her own healing process, asking her sister for help, a trained counselor. It was during the first few months of intense energy work that she had suddenly remembered why she was so angry with her ex-husband—it was a carryover from several major past-life betrayals for which she had not forgiven him. As soon as she had healed this chunk of her own emotional baggage, their reason for being together ended, and they split up. Though it was difficult at the time, now she was thankful to him for pushing her into getting help with her healing.

Plus, she was now convinced that everyone (except for perhaps very new souls) at some point in their lives must address their anger if they want to evolve as a soul. Though some people claimed not to have any anger, it was inside, repressed, and waiting for the time it could be expressed, if it hadn't yet been healed. She believed that this repressed emotional energy was a rampant problem on the planet now, and the cause of much of the violence and misplaced frustration and upsets. But she hadn't been able to convince Omaran of this—that it was all right for spiritual people to express these emotions, as long as they released them safely. That was the part he didn't get, the part about releasing them safely and without blame. And Omaran's rage was different than hers had been, because she knew he wasn't really mad at her—they had no karma between them to work out.

Understanding how it felt to be angry did help her remain somewhat detached at times, so she could observe Omaran's behavior better. The first thing she noticed was that the things he said when he was angry or irritated were the same things, over and over, as if he were playing a looped tape from the past. The repeated phrases didn't vary much from time to time, and they had nothing to do with what was going on in the present. Sometimes she was able to predict what he would say next.

When, during one of his lucid periods, she told him she had figured out that he was saying the same things over and over, he did listen to her.

"You mean, I say the same things every time I get upset?"

"Yes, there are phrases you tend to repeat, and they really have nothing to do with the current situation. They are like tapes from the past kicking in, loops of words."

He considered this. "Like what?"

Using her best imitation, she voiced a few she could remember. That really hit home. He thought about it seriously afterwards. Could he be reacting from events in the past, and is that why he was getting so angry over things that really were not worth getting angry about? Was he just overreacting because he was still angry from before? Maybe even from long ago, in previous lifetimes? The Council had told him that, and it sounded true. But he didn't know how to break out of the pattern, how to stop himself. The hateful words just came out without his being able to control them. He really did not want to be that way, but it seemed that the programming was too strong.

Antera also noticed that the different tapes had personalities associated with them, and she started calling them his "demons." When she did that, he got even more furious, not wanting to think that he had evil entities as part of him. But for her, it aptly described what she perceived to be his sub-personalities, as well as the dark energy that surrounded him when he lost control; plus the fact that he remembered very little of what they said afterwards. It was as if he just stepped aside and let the demons say and do what they wanted.

Her attempts to bring him back to present time mostly failed. She tried many different approaches, and usually had to simply stop talking to him and in a few hours he would return to coherency by himself. Since he couldn't cry it out, she suggested he yell, hit pillows, whatever it took to get the energy out without aiming it at her. But he just didn't seem to understand. At least he didn't hit her, she thought, though he really tried to look as threatening as possible at times.

One afternoon, he came at her in his most threatening demon-mode, while she was sitting by the fire pit at their campsite, reading. She instinctively crossed her two index fingers as a sign of the cross and held them up at him for protection. This took him aback, and he stopped. He thought it meant that she was "hexing" him somehow. He picked up her cherished coffee mug and threw it as far as he could before stomping off into the woods.

After briskly walking through the woods and brush for a while, he no longer felt the fight-or-flight energy cursing through his veins, so he found a comfortable spot and sat down, leaning against a fir tree. He closed his eyes for a moment, and called all the angels and beings of Light he could think of, for help. This anger was out of hand and he knew he needed help. He couldn't even remember now why he had gotten so upset just half an hour before, and this was happening way too much of the time.

Please help me control or release this anger. What is wrong with me? He prayed. As far back as he could remember, these uncontrollable angry spells had taken him over occasionally, but never this often. *Spiritual people aren't supposed to be that way, they are supposed to be calm and loving and gentle.*

That thought made him feel even worse, even more like a fake. He was really not ready for all of this spiritual work. Antera seemed to have it all together, she had been doing this all her life, she had worked for decades on clearing her emotional body. She had her guides to talk to. And here he was, pretending to be at the same level as her! How could they possibly be twin flames? There was no way he could work on healing for decades, there had to be an easier way! He just had to get control! Maybe he could be nice if he just tried really hard. . . .

He suddenly remembered throwing Antera's cup, and felt badly about it. She was very fond of it, and now it was undoubtedly broken, if he could even find it in the brush. He decided to buy her a new one and offer it to her as a gesture of making up.

Walking sheepishly, he made his way back to camp—after all, there was no other place to go—not saying anything to Antera when he got there. She was still sitting by the campfire reading, and didn't even look up. He could see her tear-streaked face when he glanced over. He hated apologizing because it seemed like he was doing it every day now. He got out a book and sat in his chair without a word.

After a few minutes of silence, she looked up, took a deep breath, and ventured, "I really don't know what to do with you. I never know whether you are going to be nice or mean from one moment to the next. I just can't live this way."

"Then why do you stay with me if I'm so awful?"

"Right now, I have no other place to go or I probably would be gone. But my guidance says you are worth sticking around for, as long as you are making efforts to heal. They are trying to talk me into staying . . . you know, they seem to think you are pretty dang special." She watched his reaction to that carefully.

He looked very sad. "Well I'm obviously letting them and everyone down. I want to control the anger but I just can't do it. It comes up so quickly and I spiral into the abyss. . . . I'm not worthy of their attention, and maybe I'll never heal."

She sighed. It seemed like she was sighing a lot lately, taking deep breaths as if the oxygen would soothe her insides. "Please listen to me carefully. I'm not your enemy. I've never attacked you in any way, I've never harmed you or said mean things, I've only given you love. But you keep treating me as if I were attacking you, as if I were your mortal enemy. What will it take for you to see that I'm not anyone from your past? I'm not your enemy!"

He thought about that. "You're right, you have never been mean or attacked me. You only love me. But sometimes it just *seems* like I'm being attacked, and I get upset. Are you saying that you think I get upset because you remind me of my ex?"

"Why else would you react as if I were your enemy? I know you were abused."

"I wasn't abused, just criticized a lot."

"Love, that is called emotional abuse. That is exactly what emotional abuse is all about, and it is almost as damaging as being physically abused."

"It is?" He thought that over. It had never occurred to him that he had been abused. He had grown so used to a combative relationship in his previous marriage that it had seemed normal to him, even if it wasn't comfortable. And to be honest, it had been a two-way battle. He didn't blame his ex-wife. He had learned to defend himself and dish the criticism right back. Anyway, he thought he'd healed his past relationships, after that ceremony he did on Mt. Tamalpais last year. Could there be still more pain from that? Was it never ending? It was something to think about.

He said, "Maybe you're right about reminding me of someone in my past. I seem to get angry when you ask me questions, even though they are innocent questions. That may be because I expect questions to be loaded with judgment and criticism; ones that would try to make me feel bad." He thought more about how painful that time of his life had been. "Maybe I still expect the underlying put-downs, even though deep inside I know you are not being critical."

She felt his pain. "It's terrible that you had to go through that. Why in the world did you stay in the relationship so long?"

"I guess out of fear. I was afraid I'd lose the kids. So I stayed many years longer than I should have. Looking back, it is easy to see that, but at the time, I just didn't have the courage to leave, I guess." Thinking about that made him feel even worse, especially because of the effect those choices were now having on his current relationship. These were new revelations for him.

Antera felt compassion for him, understanding how difficult it must have been. But she needed to get back to the problems at hand. "Hopefully, thinking about the reasons you react as you do will help you gain more control, because this is a far cry from my idea of a loving relationship with my twin flame. I expect you to love me, and allow me to love you. I expect any problems that come up to be talked about in a civil manner with respect for each other at all times. I expect to be able to work together to find the deeper cause of any upsets that come up, to release them without any harm to each other, so we can maintain clear energy flow between us always . . . ALWAYS! It is intolerable for me to have energy barriers between us. We are too close . . . whether you think we are twin flames or not!"

He winced at that last statement, knowing that he had more than once denied their twin-flame connection during his angry episodes, despite the fact that he truly didn't have any doubts about it. He didn't want to keep saying things that he didn't mean or even believe. Staring at the fire pit and the ashes from last night's fire, he said, "That sounds reasonable. I just don't know that I can do it. Maybe we got together too soon, and I should have done more healing first."

She shook her head. "Frankly, I don't think this would even come up to be healed if you weren't with me. You would have kept that energy buried as long as you could. It's natural for human beings to try and avoid pain. But in intimate soul-based relationships, you can't hide anything, and heal you must."

"Hmmm." He looked across the valley through the trees, noticing that the sun was going down and how beautiful the sky in the west was. Bright salmon-colored streaks of clouds stretched across the wide vista. With all his heart and soul he wanted to heal, he wanted to have that kind of loving relationship with her. Was it really possible? He wasn't convinced. What happened to "happily ever after" with soulmates? He never thought soulmates would have to work hard to live together happily. He reminded himself to breathe deeply.

She went on, "Look, I simply need something to keep me going. I need to know that you are really trying to gain control, and that you are trying to release that energy harmlessly, and that you are putting it at the top of your priority list."

He slowly turned to look at her for the first time since sitting down. "I can't promise that, I can only say I'll try. Is that good enough?"

"No, I need some kind of agreement from you so I know you are trying, something concrete. How about doing what the Council suggested months ago, and agreeing to sit in meditation whenever you get angry, at the first sign? Then concentrate on opening your heart. That is a good way to get perspective and stop the cycle long enough so you can look at the real issues before saying things you will have to apologize for later." She didn't think he would do it even now, but it was worth a try.

"OK," he said slowly, thinking it over. "I'll try to do that."

"Try?"

"I can't promise anything! All I can do is try. You are asking too much if you think I can suddenly change like that. You need to be more patient, and give me more time."

"This is far from sudden, you've had months to get this together. Saying you'll try just gives you a way out."

"I really will do my best. I think it is a good idea."

"If that is the best you can do, we'll see how it goes. I'm sure you'll have a chance to try it soon," she said fatefully. She didn't have her hopes up. His pattern was to say anything to end these kinds of discussions, then later forget all about what they had decided, and what agreements they had made.

The energy wasn't settled between them, and that probably would take a while. But he did put forth a bigger effort to control his anger for a while after that. A number of times he sat down and got quiet when he was feeling upset, and got a message regarding what he was really upset about—something in the past, and not what he had thought. This was progress, if he would keep it up.

They still enjoyed their daily hikes and adventures, and while he was out hiking, he was almost always on good behavior. It seemed to keep him happy. Antera couldn't shun him for long because they had so much fun together when he was lucid. But she didn't want him to think that how he had acted was OK or easily forgotten, either.

Fourteen

High places are calling me,
calling me to climb,
up to where I know I'm free,
I know I'll meet the Divine.
I know I'll meet the Divine.

— From the song
"High Places"

One day while in town for some errands and laundry, they called and arranged to meet Peter, one of the few people they knew in town, at a coffee shop later that day. They had met him last April when they came up for the weekend, and attended a local event in town. At that time, he had come up to them and commented that he could feel that they were full of the Christ Light, and there had been an instant rapport between the three of them as if they were old friends from long ago. He was a wise old soul, in his 60s, with a perennial smile in his eyes and a slow-talking style that reminded Antera of her Texan grandfather.

They saw him as they entered the Bagel Café, a small but popular breakfast and lunch spot, and went over to hug. After placing their orders for lunch, they sat at a table by the window.

"So, how've you been?" Omaran asked, glad to see him.

"Oh, pretty good, my healing work is keeping me fairly busy." He told them about some of his current clients without revealing names.

Omaran was intrigued by the laying on of hands that Peter did, because his own hands also had a lot of energy flowing from them and

113

he had often wondered if he could develop that flow to help people in the same way. He asked Peter, "So how did you start this healing practice, anyway? How did you find out that you could heal? Did you get trained?"

Peter chuckled at his exuberance, light filling his eyes. "I'll tell you how it started, but you may not believe it."

"Oh, we've heard and seen some strange things—please tell us," Antera invited.

Peter loved telling stories, and he took his time. "Well, about five years ago, a couple of friends and I climbed the mountain. We trained for it for weeks by hiking up Black Butte and other places around here where there is a good elevation change. I was drawn up there by Spirit, like I simply had to go to the top, to get the energy up there. So we picked the date, and went even though the weather wasn't perfect. It was a hard journey."

Omaran told him, "I know, I've climbed it twice and once we were whited out just a couple hundred feet from the top and had to turn back."

"Yes, that happens sometimes, and if the mountain doesn't want you there, it will make sure you don't get there. Well, we made it to the top, but it turned out that a strange thunderstorm appeared when we reached the summit . . . lightning and thunder all around us. The electric charge was very strong, and I could feel it. The others took cover, but I went to the very highest point and stood there. I could see blue static electricity sparking between the fingers of my hands when I opened them, and my hair stood on end. My whole body felt like I was being set up for a lightning strike, with intense electric charge all through it. My friends yelled at me to come down, but I was enjoying it, laughing gleefully. I imagine I looked like a character in a cartoon that sticks a nail into an electrical outlet and gets shocked. I figured that if I was to die, that would be a great place to do it."

"Did lightning strike?" Omaran asked.

"No, but the voltage that went through my body was tremendous. I think it opened up something in my nervous system, and especially in my hands." He paused as the waitress brought their lunches to the table.

The three of them thanked the waitress, and started eating. Peter continued. "So anyway, a few days later, when a friend of mine tripped and hurt her foot, she asked me to hold it. I looked at it and the bones of some of her toes were obviously broken and hanging out of line. So I put her foot between my hands and asked for the masters to heal it through me. I held it for about 20 minutes, feeling an unusually large flow of energy through my hands, and when I let go the bones were perfect and there was no pain, as if it had never happened. She was amazed, and started telling others that I had healed her. Of course, I told her that it wasn't me, but the energy of God flowing through me. So that is how it started. I think my hands were opened up by Mt. Shasta."

"What a great story!" Antera enjoyed it, not caring whether it was slightly exaggerated or not. Many people they had met on the mountain had fantastic stories to tell, right on the edge of reality—and probably some of their own stories would seem incredulous to others as well.

They talked more about the mountain and its energy, how the two of them had been so drawn there for the summer, and all the hiking they had done so far.

Peter said, "Oh, you like to hike? I know where four power spots are, with medicine wheels, one on each side of the mountain. You have to hike to three of them. Want me to take you there?"

They were excited about having a tour of power spots, especially in light of their recently-acquired memories of being land healers in Lemuria. So they arranged to meet the following day to journey first to the one which was farthest away, on the eastern side of the mountain.

Within one week, they went to all the spots Peter had told them about, the three of them cramming into the front seat of Omaran's truck and driving as far as they could on dirt roads, then hiking the rest of the way. They compared their experiences with each other, each of them sensing the energy in different ways. Peter felt his hands buzz when he approached the concentration of power at these places, and was able to find their boundaries by walking around them and sensing with his hands. Omaran tended to feel lightheaded and a bit dizzy in them, and Antera felt the energy rushing up or down her spine and in her head.

Near each power spot, a medicine wheel had been built and was maintained by hikers who occasionally visited them. These were circles made of rocks, with a cross inside aligned with the compass directions. Called vortexes because of the spiraling energy flow, they each had a little different feel. The energy flow was outward or inward, rather than horizontal as in most land areas, as if the Earth were letting extra energy out or pulling it in.

They found the vortex on the east side to be the most raw, perhaps because it was the least visited by people. While sitting within it, Antera felt herself being sucked down in a spiraling motion into the depths of the Earth, and then suddenly pushed out like on a fountain to fly high above it. It was a wild ride at first, but after they had been there a while the energy settled and she could keep her consciousness in the middle at ground level.

It seemed perfectly natural for the three of them to be doing this kind of work together—and it was work, for the vortices did need harmonizing and healing—and they could all feel that there was a purpose to their visits, and good reasons that Spirit had brought them together.

In the evenings, the Council instructed Antera and Omaran in what they could do at the power spots, for the maximum healing effect. From deep down, they were to bring the energy out of the Earth, raw energy that needed to be vented, and mix it with the Christ Light from above, using their bodies as the place of union. This process stabilized, harmonized and balanced the energy of the area. They started incorporating this kind of land healing in their hikes as well, harmonizing any areas that felt in need. They were grateful to Peter for giving them an opportunity to understand more of their Earth healing work. The memories and skills from that far-away time in Lemuria, when they had done similar, though much more sophisticated work together, were further reawakened.

Peter's story about being "charged up" at the summit instilled in Omaran a desire to climb the mountain again. When he had done it years before with some of his buddies, the focus of the climbs had been mostly about the physical and mental challenge of conquering the mountain. Now that he was more sensitive to energy and more consciously aware of Spirit, he knew such a trek would be a much deeper spiritual experience.

He really wanted Antera to go also, but she didn't have any inclination to do so, especially since she had experienced terrible altitude sickness when she had climbed Mt. Whitney, the highest peak in the continental U.S., a few years before, and it was only a couple of hundred feet higher than Shasta. So he didn't push her, but kept pointing out the climbers they could see through binoculars from the campsite, describing the route most people took.

One day, while she was sitting in her chair by the fire pit looking up at the peak, she remarked that it really didn't look very far to the top. Omaran suddenly got very excited, but was able to hide it because he was standing behind her. He knew she would have to make the decision to climb herself, and any push on his part may only turn her away.

He made it sound as easy as possible. "No, it really isn't far. Just a one day trip, up and back."

"It doesn't look all that hard, really," she said. "The top is just right there, I can see it."

"Well . . . it's a tough climb. I mean a lot of people do it, but it's tough."

"Why?"

"It's just a lot of UP," he replied.

"We've been going on hikes every day, and they always have some up."

He could see that she was considering it. "Climbing Shasta is more. I think we could do it, though. Our bodies are in good shape."

She asked some more questions about the climb, and he answered with a casual air. And sure enough, the seed took hold and she slowly warmed to the idea over a few days' time. She then actually agreed to go.

The real turning point in her decision came after they hiked up to Horse Camp, a Sierra Club hut at 8000 feet. On the way down, they were both so charged with energy that they started running and laughing, and kept it up all the way back to the truck, even though they were wearing boots and small backpacks that pounded their backs with each step. They weren't even winded after the run, and agreed that the mountain must have given them the extra energy. Omaran also convinced her that because they were camping at 6000 feet and hiking at relatively high altitudes daily, she wouldn't have as hard a time with the altitude as she previously had when she went directly from sea level to the peak of Mt. Whitney.

So they rented ice axes and crampons, pulled together the best gear they could, and on a morning in early August at 6:00 am, they hit the trail from Sand Flat. The first light of dawn was glowing through the trees, and the full moon lit their way along the path. When the sun came up more fully, the sky was perfectly clear, a beautiful day for the hike. It was an arduous climb, but they were in good shape from all the hiking they had been doing. Peter and a friend of his had decided to go with them, but they were considerably slower, so Antera and Omaran had to leave them behind to go their own pace or they knew they would never make it themselves. Omaran led the two of them on a detour that he thought would be faster but ended up costing them an hour because they had to retrace their steps back to the main pathway up Avalanche Gulch. The snow-covered slope was so steep, especially on the detour, that their ankles and calves ached, and they only got relief by occasionally digging out holes in the snow to step in so they could stand on flat ground for a couple of minutes.

All they ate were small bites of power bars, for they had no appetite—no thirst either, but they forced themselves to drink water every half hour so they wouldn't get dehydrated. When they made it up the gulch and started up Misery Hill, Antera found out why it was called that. What they could see from their campsite was not the top, a fact that Omaran had neglected to point out. Misery Hill went on and on, and the air was so thin, above 13,000 feet, that she was panting with each step, going slower and slower. Omaran wasn't as bothered by the altitude, so he took her pack and hoped she could make it, knowing that she was pushing her body forward on will power alone. The snow was in patches, so they had to take their crampons off and on. But at last the top was in sight. As they slowly dragged their bodies up the last couple hundred feet, a large black eagle flew around them a few times then back down the slope, as if to welcome them. And there they were! It was 3:30 pm.

The sky was such a deep shade of navy blue it almost looked like outer space, evoking images of space seen from space flights, though not quite dark enough to see the stars. The rocks were twisted and white, a testament to the explosive events that created the mountain. The energy was intensely focused at the peak, stripping them to the core and then charging them up with powerful electricity. Now THIS was a real power spot! It made the energy of the others seem like the flow of tiny creeks compared with the Amazon River. They stayed at the summit for about forty-five minutes, and were glad they happened to be alone. Antera was dizzy, and couldn't tell if it was mostly from the power of the mountain or the altitude—probably a combination of both. Omaran was ecstatic.

The descent was even more difficult because their knees really took a beating—7000 feet of elevation drop, down with every step. They noticed that other climbers had taken something to slide on down the snow-covered slope, and were descending very quickly without the wear and tear on the knees. It was dark with only the moon to light their way for the last part of the trail through the woods, and at 9:30 they made it to the truck at last. They drove to the campsite and collapsed in the tent.

Most of the next day they spent horizontal in the tent, getting up only for essentials. They had prepared for this, by putting food and water close by to be easily reached. Their bodies had depleted all reserves. But it was a good tired, and they both felt a certain change in their energy fields from the peak exposure, a buzzing in all their cells. Now the mountain was really a part of them. It had drawn them there against the odds, and finally had pulled them to the top for the ultimate energy rush.

Fifteen

And as we move into the new,
Light will come
and it will lead the way.
And as we move into the Light,
new will come
and all will fall away.

— From the song
"The Light"

During the last week of their stay, the spirit of the mountain was noticeably engrained in their consciousness. It spoke to them, sang to them, meditated with them, and filled them with a sense of oneness. They were very glad they had made the trip to the top, for it seemed the perfect climax for their visit. As the time to leave grew near, they were feeling complete and ready to go back to the "real" world.

Thoughts about new projects to work on, as soon as they moved back into a house, started filling their conversation together. Not the least of these was a vision, which had emerged over the last few weeks, of creating a spiritual center and mystery school. The idea had been given to them by the angels, and had been a recurring topic of discussion throughout their sojourn here. They were excited by the possibility and wanted to start planning it right away. And there was also the second half of the Becoming a Master class to put together for the fall.

When the time came, they packed up the truck, brushed away their footprints and traces of their camp, said good bye and thanks to the animals and nature spirits, and hit the road, off to the next adventure. They watched the mountain get smaller and smaller behind them, seen for a very long way as they drove south on Interstate 5. As they got closer to the metropolis, they both started feeling heavier, as if an unseen weight had descended on them.

"Do you feel different?" Antera asked. "To me it feels like we are driving into some kind of cloud, an awful mass of energy."

"Yes, I feel uncomfortable. What do you think it is?" Omaran said.

"I'd guess it's a combination of physical, astral, and mental pollution, from having so many people in one area."

Omaran considered this concept. "But we've only been gone six weeks, could it be new? Why didn't we notice this when we lived here before? How can anyone stand to live in this?"

She shrugged. "Good question. People must get used to it. We must have been so accustomed to it before, that we didn't notice it either."

"Wow," Omaran said. "I guess we will adjust again, then. But it sure stands out now."

"I think our systems, especially our psychic senses, are extra sensitive from being on the mountain for so long," Antera said. "And it's not just the cloud, but the lack of nature that is shocking—all that pavement! What a contrast."

"Yes, I miss the forest already."

The first stop was their storage garage in San Rafael, to deposit the camping equipment and pick up some clothes, cash, and other items. To their dismay, a large, heavy lock was blocking their entry, with a note saying the rent hadn't been paid. Omaran was furious. He had paid two months in advance before leaving town, so he knew this was the manager's mistake. Unfortunately, the office was closed, so entry couldn't be gained that way. He did not let that stop him. He was determined to get in.

First, he drove to a local equipment rental place and got a pair of huge bolt cutters, the likes of which Antera had never seen. Even with Omaran's full muscle force, he couldn't do more than put small dents in the massive lock. He went back to the rental shop and returned with a very heavy three-foot sledgehammer. This produced numerous dents in the metal garage door, but the lock still held, despite the righteous anger fueling the strength of his blows.

Antera was getting a bit concerned about the damage and tried to convince him that they could wait until Monday, just two days hence, to get in, but he was unstoppable. A third trip to the shop produced a large propane torch on a cart with wheels. Antera stared at him with wide-eyed amazement, but said nothing. When he lit the torch, a two-foot long flame burst out and shot sparks all around them. "Step back!" Omaran warned, and she did. In a few seconds, the hot flame melted the lock, which flew off in a glowing mass, as well as part of the door, leaving a hole and a large scorched area.

"Ha!" He was jubilant in his success. Antera wondered if this aggressive energy had to do with the mass of dense energy they had just driven into, but didn't dare suggest it. It was quite a dramatic re-entry into the real world and this new phase of their lives.

They visited some friends in the East Bay and stayed with them the first week, while getting their bearings and going back to work. It was culture shock and energy shock to be there . . . so many people, so much pollution, so much pavement, so few trees. But they did slowly adjust. Antera's sister Janet offered them her trailer to stay in temporarily, while they searched for a house to rent, so they moved there the second week, keeping most of their belongings in storage. Janet, a petite brunette, was a musician and recording engineer who, in her twenties, had played bass guitar in an all-girl rock band. She lived in Petaluma, a small town north of Marin County.

The commute to work was an hour each way for Antera, across the bridge to the East Bay. Parked in the driveway, the small trailer was close quarters for the couple but actually larger than the tent they had been sleeping in, and they were glad for it. It was quite a challenge for Antera and Omaran to maintain their high level of energy in Petaluma. Their task was to bring the Light even here, into an area that was very dense, almost as if they were positioned in a place that was the opposite of Shasta. They tried to have faith that they were here for a good reason, and that the delays were for the higher good.

Despite the energy interference, they were able to keep a column of Light stabilized around the trailer so Antera could connect with the angels and masters. New masters unexpectedly came in verbally, presumably, she thought, because she was attuned to their higher frequencies after being in the midst of the Shasta vortex for so long. Teachers such as Jesus, Mother Mary, and Archangel Metatron came through verbally for the first time, among others. Their council was very comforting and healing, as well as stimulating. Information about the spiritual center and mystery school they were being asked to create was a favorite topic, providing the couple with plenty to talk about and plan.

Being with her sister Janet was a joy to Antera, and made being there more tolerable. The two sisters had always been close, as soulmates. Janet had more contact with "normal" people than Antera had ever had, and she tended to be a practical, grounding influence. It was Janet who suggested to the couple that their ideas were not really mainstream, and to not expect a majority of the population to be interested in the work they were doing.

"Do you have any idea how far out you are?" Janet ventured one day as they were discussing spiritual experiences.

"No, I guess not." Antera replied thoughtfully.

"Well, let me tell you, you are WAY out there compared with the rest of humanity! I hope you don't go around talking to ordinary people about ascended masters, healing the soul, past lives and other subjects that WE talk about. Most people just don't think about that kind of thing, you know?"

"I guess I've never been around ordinary people much, then."

"You've always been out there, Sis. I can count on you to keep me apprised of the cutting edge." They both laughed, knowing that Janet wasn't exactly mainstream either.

Finding a house to rent in the extremely tight market proved to be quite a challenge. After over a month of unsuccessful searching, Omaran and Antera were guided to write up a list of all the amenities they were looking for, being very specific, and even decided to set a date one month ahead for a deadline: October 31. They put this into the specific form of a Huna prayer, a method of manifestation from ancient teachings taught by the Kahunas in Hawaii. They each read the prayer request aloud three times, twice a day. There were very few houses within their price range, and they had discovered that the ones they saw in the paper were usually rented by the time the paper came out. Still, they continued with their prayer request.

When the last weekend in October came around and they had not found anything yet, Omaran suggested that they extend the deadline on their prayer. Perhaps it was not fair to ask the universe to provide something so nearly impossible in such a short time.

"What?" Antera was incredulous. "What are you saying? Have you lost your faith? There are still two days left and I just know that something will come up because we have asked very specifically."

He conceded. *She's right*, he thought. *I need to maintain my faith and not give up early.* He had wanted to give the universe a way out, as if they were asking for too much and Spirit couldn't provide. Spirit could do miracles! But the time was almost up, and he admitted, if only to himself, that he was worried.

On Sunday morning, the last day of October, Antera went to look at a place in Mill Valley that was just listed. It was a very old, small, three-bedroom house with uneven floors, but which was surrounded on all sides by a circle of stately redwood trees. The trees' presence made the energy acceptable to Antera, like a tiny island of clear space within the area. The house was nestled on the side of a hill, at the base of Mt. Tamalpais, and a creek flowed in the back yard among pear, apple and cherry trees.

The owners happened to be there when she went to see it, finishing up some remodeling they had been doing after the last tenants, including new carpets and paint. They talked for a bit and Antera said she would bring her partner back. She paged Omaran, and he called her back on a pay phone in the main plaza, then came quickly over. They filled out the application on the spot, and it was placed on a large pile of other applications.

That very evening they got a call from the owners. "You can have the house if you want it," they told Omaran.

It had only been a few hours—it was unheard of to rent without doing the usual credit check and calling of references, and there hadn't been time! Plus, there had been quite a stack of other applicants. Omaran tried to act cool as he told them they would take it, and be by tomorrow to sign a lease.

Excitedly, he hung up and told the two sisters, "I can't believe it! On the evening of the very last day of our prayer we got the house we asked for! They didn't even check us out, and said they decided for once to go on their gut feeling. Is that amazing or what?"

Janet was impressed and decided to try the method for some things she wanted. Antera was relieved that their prayer had worked, reaffirming all of their faiths. At last, to be in a real house again! And at the base of Mt. Tam!

Sixteen

Other times and other places
you and me, we had different faces.
I wonder if you can see.
Do you remember me?

— From the song
"Do You Remember Me?"

The move and settling in to the new house took a lot of their energy, but when they were comfortable again, focus shifted to other things. They were being trained in many processes and tools very quickly, some for their own healing and soul evolution, and others for the future work of the spiritual center. It was all coming into their lives very fast, and it was an exciting time for them.

Archangel Metatron started regular teachings on frequencies and geometrical forms. This included an introduction to flower essences, which turned out to be the most effective tools for physical and emotional healing they had yet received. They started using sets of essences made by Perelandra, a nature research center in Virginia, and found that they helped them remain mentally, emotionally, and physically balanced, working on the subtle bodies through the electrical and nervous systems.

Only a month after they started using them, Metatron asked them to make their own set of essences from trees on Mt. Tamalpais on which he was bestowing a special blessing, a Divine dispensation. The essences were to be for lightworkers, to help them bring in and integrate the new frequencies on the planet. It sounded like a fun project, so they said yes.

As in all their projects, there were personal lessons to be learned in the process. When they were told that they had to find the eight individual trees that were given the blessing, Omaran started feeling very nervous about locating the right ones. How would they be guided to them? Mt. Tamalpais was a vast place. He had been hiking on the mountain for almost two decades, and was well acquainted with its trails. So he knew that it would mostly be his job to find the trees. His fears of failure came up, and his faith in his own guidance was tested; nevertheless, they had accepted the challenge, and went ahead full force.

They hiked on the mountain almost every weekend throughout the winter, so they could find the trees before they flowered in the spring, which could be as early as February for some. Omaran's sense of place was very strong, though so much a part of him that he didn't recognize it as a unique skill. Many times when he had a hunch to hike to particular areas, as if they were calling him, he walked right to a tree that telepathically let him or Antera know that it was a participant. A couple of the trees even presented themselves to him in dreams, and told him of their whereabouts. So finding the trees wasn't as difficult as he had thought, and this helped to build faith in his intuition, and dissipate his fears. It became more like a treasure hunt.

After finding the trees, they needed to continue to visit them to monitor the timing of the blooms, so they did a lot of hiking, which was one of their favorite things to do together. When they made the essences, special care was taken in each step, as they considered it sacred work. They stayed by the trees while the energy of the flowers and the sun was being infused into the water. While sitting there in meditation, Antera discovered that she could clearly hear the tree spirits speaking to her, explaining the gift that the essences would be imparting to lightworkers. They told her what to use them for, and what qualities would be enhanced by each of them.

Metatron's teachings on sacred geometry, during this time, were centered on the effect of various forms on the human-spirit energy field. Some of these teachings were carried out in the inner planes during channeled sessions, when they were asked to imagine different shapes around them, such as cubes, rectangles, spheres, and pyramids, and assess how their energy changed.

Other lessons were given during the night while their bodies slept, when they found themselves in training sessions with Metatron and other master teachers. They would awaken in the morning with only partial memories, which fled quickly if they didn't make the effort to grab at them by writing the experiences down or talking about them. The nighttime training was intense, and they were learning skills that could not be entirely grasped with their waking minds. Vaguely, they knew they were working with shapes made entirely of Light, and forming various geometrical patterns with balls and lines of Light, for specific purposes. Antera remembered more than Omaran from these classes, but when she talked about what the training was, he often could remember being there as well.

An opportunity was soon magically arranged for them to experience the geometrical forms more physically. One day in February, almost four months after moving, Antera was cleaning out a stack of old flyers and came across a pamphlet someone had given her three years before. It was about what was called "energy acceleration devices," and as she read it a strong pull told her it was time to follow up.

She called the number and a man named Steven asked her a lot of questions about her spiritual practice, explaining that he only works with people who are energy sensitive and ready for the experience.

Steven came to their home a few days later to give them each an energy session. A small man with a New York accent, dark hair with a few gray streaks, and a full beard greeted them at the door. He had a no-nonsense approach and was very serious about his work, which he held as sacred, but his laugh was readily forthcoming in conversation—a loud, infectious laugh that was delightful and from the gut. They immediately took to him as a soul brother.

Steven opened his bag of goods, and brought out several of the containers, impressively organized and well packed. "Now I'll be honest with you, I don't know exactly how these work," he said. "I can't feel energy at all. I've tried for many years, and finally accepted that I am not supposed to feel this, or I wouldn't be able to do this work, and be exposed to these for such long periods of time. So, I depend on people like you who can feel energy flow to tell me what they are doing to the human energy field. I have several people who are very tuned into them and who test them for me each time I make a new one."

"You've never felt these? I can feel my whole body buzzing just from you opening the bag," Antera said. "I guess being around them all the time would make it difficult to do anything else if you were sensitive, so that makes sense."

"Yes. So I keep a notebook and record all the perceptions of people who sit with them, continuing to gather data. I'm very analytical by nature, so that job suits me. And by the way, you'll only need to experience these particular ones once in your lifetime, no more. They do their job and that is it."

He took the first one out of its plastic container, and unwrapped a piece of silk that was covering it. Sized to easily fit into the palm of a hand, it was a delicate piece made of copper wire and crystals, in complicated geometrical configurations. The numerous tiny double-terminated crystals were wrapped or soldered into the wire form, obviously positioned with great accuracy. Omaran was impressed with the quality of the work that went into making it. Antera was immediately reminded of the Light forms they had been studying in their nighttime training classes. They both said, "Wow."

"I wrap them in silk for storage and clean them with it after each session, because I'm told that is needed to keep their energy pure. So the way this one is used, you sit and hold it this way. The energy should rise, do its job, then subside when it is done. I appreciate it if you describe what you are feeling during the process. Which of you wants to be first?"

Antera said she would go first, anxious to hold the device that she could already feel uplifting her energy. He handed it to her and sat quietly watching while she closed her eyes. First, the energy became more intense as it was activated, like it suddenly came alive, and she felt like she was in another dimension entirely, another space. Then a being appeared.

"Oh! I see someone, she is a crystal goddess! She is very beautiful, transparent like a quartz crystal . . . she says she is the deva, or angel, in charge of the device, and she is directing the energy work."

It was the first time Antera had actually perceived such a fascinating being so clearly, and she was delighted. The deva concentrated on the area between the third and fourth chakras, the balance point between higher and lower energy centers, which was the focus of this device. When this area was balanced and cleared, she disappeared and the energy seemed to shut down, bringing Antera back into the room.

"That was really neat!" She exclaimed as she passed it to her mate.

"Wait! I have to clean it first," Steven intercepted the device and cleared its energy with a silk cloth before handing it to Omaran.

Omaran felt the energy very strongly as well, in his own way. He described what he was feeling to Steven, who occasionally prompted him in a quiet voice. He saw colors and Light flashing around him, and a sensation of being cleared of old, stuck energy from the past that was no longer needed.

In a similar way, they went through five different devices in a specific order, each building on what the previous one had accomplished. They were all made of the same materials and were of a hand-held size, but they differed in shape and purpose, working on different areas of the energy body. The session lasted about three hours, after which Steven packed up to leave, to allow them time to integrate the experience.

He paused at the door and asked, "So, if you don't mind me asking, are those your real names?"

Omaran laughed. "Yes, these are our spiritual names, and we changed them legally."

"And you only have one name each? No last name?" Steven asked.

"Only one," Antera answered, "and it sure has caused more difficulties than we thought it would. You should hear some of the things people say. Some people actually think it is illegal to only have one name, or act like we are trying to hide something."

Omaran added, "And many databases require two names, so we have seen some very imaginative last names added on. I've actually gotten mail addressed to 'Omaran Goesby' and 'Omaran NA.' But my favorite was 'Omaran Idonthaveone.'"

Steven laughed. "How funny. I think it is really neat that you are using your spiritual names. Well, let me know how you feel over the next few days." And he left.

They felt a tremendous sense of peace, yet with a sparkle of increased Light. An afterglow of overall well-being lasted for a few days. When Omaran called Steven to tell him of these beneficial effects, he offered to put them through another sequence the next week. They were excited.

The second session consisted of three devices that balanced the internal male and female aspects. Steven said, "These haven't had as much research done with them, only a few people have tried them, so please give me your feedback." Again he patiently sat as they used them, and they both had profound experiences. Antera conversed with the Crystal Deva again and then had a flashback to a past life.

"I just had a vision about devices like these in the temples of Atlantis," she described for the men. "We were in an important meeting about them, the three of us with maybe eight or ten others. We were wearing robes. It seems that devices similar to these, but some of them bigger, were used in the initiations and training there. But they were kept very secret, because we knew that they were not beneficial for people who weren't spiritually ready for them, and plus, in the wrong hands they could be used for harmful purposes.

"We were discussing how one person had betrayed the trust of the group and allowed their use by others with harmful or ignorant motives, and this had created major problems. Now they had to be hidden. We had to decide how to deal with it, how to protect the rest of the devices so they would not fall into the wrong hands. We tried to hide them, but somehow I don't think we were entirely successful. Very interesting."

"So, the three of us have worked together before with these kinds of instruments! That is not surprising," Omaran said. "We are so naturally attracted to them, as if we had used them before."

Steven laughed. "Well, I'm no longer surprised with what Spirit brings together. Something is always being planned, like us meeting each other now. There is always a deeper purpose. I had a feeling that these kinds of energy accelerators were used in Atlantis."

After this session, Omaran and Antera felt good but a little restless, so they didn't sleep well. A lot of energy had been imparted and their nervous systems were challenged to integrate it all. They were advised by Metatron to do a lot of stretching and yoga, to open the energy pathways and move the energy, and this alleviated the problem, so they could feel the expanded state their energy was in and be harmonized with it once again.

After the formal session work, Steven came over occasionally to experiment with new devices he created, or just to visit. He also started attending the weekly meditations in their home. He became a good friend, and they liked his eccentric personality, laughing a lot when together. They could all relate to each other's experiences and trials on the spiritual path. On one of his visits, he showed them pictures of some larger devices he had. They were immediately attracted to them.

"Wow, you mean you can sit right inside these? That sounds really neat." Omaran said as they looked at the pictures.

"Yes, they aren't portable, as you can see, so I can't take them around for people to experience. My apartment isn't large enough to put them up, so right now I have them carefully packed away in storage."

"What a shame! I'd like to try them. I like the idea of being totally surrounded by the geometrical forms and crystals." Antera said.

"Yes," Steven agreed, "my ex-wife and I used to have them set up right in our living room. It was quite a sight for people coming over, but hey, we didn't care. They are very powerful, but now that I am in a smaller apartment, they aren't being used. That's why I developed these smaller, hand-held ones. Just thought you'd like to see them." He put the pictures away, but that wasn't to be the last they saw of them.

Metatron had plans. He told Antera and Omaran a few days later, in a channeling session, that the large devices would soon be transferred to them—that they were to be the new guardians of the ancient devices. He confirmed that they were similar to the ones used long ago on Atlantis in the temples, and said that they would be coming into renewed life at the spiritual center they were creating. But he asked them not to tell Steven about this, because he would have to come to that decision himself. So they waited to see what would develop, and didn't think much about it.

It was several months later that Steven casually asked them if they would like to take possession of the large devices. "They are just taking up space in my storage area, and maybe you two can find a place to set them up and put them to use again."

"Are you serious?" Omaran asked, once again astounded by what the masters were able to arrange.

"Well, Spirit tells me that it is time to pass them on, that they need new guardians. My time with them is up. It is a responsibility, you know, to keep these—not to be taken lightly." Steven said seriously.

"Of course we'd love to have them, but we'd need to do something for you in exchange. We know how monetarily valuable they are and wouldn't feel right without a flow back to you, some kind of compensation," Antera said.

"It is Spirit's desire that you have them, so nothing is needed. For all we know, maybe this is a pay-back of a debt from another lifetime or something."

Antera looked at Omaran and he said, "Well, maybe something will come up so we can help you in some way . . . perhaps when you finally move we can help with that."

Steven had been planning a move out of the Bay Area for a long time, but the opportunity hadn't yet manifested. He said, "That sounds reasonable. Sure, it's a deal."

Omaran asked Antera, "Should we tell him what Metatron told us a few months ago?"

"I guess so."

He told Steven about Metatron's message that said the large devices would be transferred to them, the new guardians.

Steven was astounded. "Ha! That is just how Spirit works. Always setting these things up. Well then, there you go! It is good to have confirmation that we are doing the right thing. Did Metatron say anything else about them? He's a heavy hitter, so I really listen to what he says."

They shared other aspects of what they had received from the Archangel, and continued to tell Steven of other messages that came through that pertained to him over the next few months. They all had a good laugh when Metatron commented on being called a "heavy hitter," saying that he preferred to be called a "Light hitter."

And so they became the keepers of the devices. They were to be used in the future mystery school. In the meantime, Omaran made a room for them by converting an old greenhouse in the back yard, and they experimented with them on themselves and some friends. Antera was able to communicate to the spirit in charge of each one, and was told their purpose, which apparently had changed slightly from when they were being used by the previous owners. By using them themselves, they felt their own energy opened and tuned to higher spiritual frequencies, and their inner senses getting stronger.

Another part of their intensive instruction on forms and sacred geometry focused on crystals and the basic pyramid shape. They experimented with arrangements of crystals around them, using them for various healing purposes and to access certain transformational spaces. Omaran built a small pyramid out of copper tubing that was just large enough to sit inside, and they set it up in the middle of their living room while they experimented with it.

The first time they tried it out, they could feel a shaft of Light right down the center of the spine, through the central core of their energy, opening and purging it. It seemed to rejuvenate the physical body, and make their hands buzz with energy. It also seemed to loosen up emotional issues to be healed. Omaran felt cranky when he got out, and Antera started laughing uproariously, suddenly finding it very comical that they had a pyramid in their living room! The laughter was catching, so Omaran joined in and they both had a great release that relieved the tension in a fun and harmless way.

They experimented quite a lot with the pyramid, even sleeping inside it for a week, during which time they had unusual dreams and nighttime experiences. Their natural sense of exploration with the devices and the pyramid, plus a host of smaller pyramids made from cardboard that they put on their chakras to balance them, entertained them for many hours over the weeks.

Once, while driving on the freeway to a friend's house, they were wearing brightly-colored pyramids on their heads, with strings holding them in place, like hats. At first, they talked about how it was affecting their energy and making them feel very alert. After about 20 minutes, they had quite forgotten about them and were having casual conversation, when they noticed a car in the next lane speeding up, then slowing down, as if to get their attention. When they looked over, a man was grinning broadly at them, and giving them an enthusiastic thumbs-up, pointing to his head. They waved, and only then realized that he was looking at their pyramids, and that set them to laughing, realizing how silly it must look to others. They remembered to take them off before going inside a store on the way to their destination.

Though this was a time of tremendous spiritual growth and exploration for them, the underlying tension from Omaran's anger continued to be a threat to their joy. The accelerated growth he was experiencing continued to bring up his deep pain to be healed, which meant addressing his demons. Or else lose it all.

Seventeen

Shake off your demons,
get in control.
I'm not your enemy,
I'm here to love you.
Call back your offense,
your defense too.
I don't want to fight,
I'm here to heal you.

— From the song
"Please Just Love Me"

The good times they had together were occasionally punctuated by angry explosions, as Omaran couldn't yet control or release his rage safely. Antera still found loving him during these attacks very difficult. In fact, her tolerance was growing thinner and thinner. Her guidance kept reminding her, during this time, that everything the demons said were lies. None of it had to do with her, it was unresolved material from his past. Continually reminding herself of this fact helped her deal with these trying times. Indeed, when Omaran came back to his senses after these episodes, he always apologized and said he didn't mean what he had said—and didn't remember most of it.

So she tried to recognize as soon as possible when the demon presence appeared, because it could come up, from her perspective, very subtly and unexpectedly. As soon as she felt the now-familiar energy field, she would say, "I'm not going to talk to you now because Omaran is no longer present. Everything you say is lies and I don't believe a word of it. We'll talk when Omaran is back and can talk to me with love and respect."

Of course, this got him/them even more angry, but she would leave the room or the house, if necessary, to get away. She found that if she did not talk to him at all during these times, Omaran came back to present time much more quickly. The demons needed someone to talk to, yell at, and hate. So if she refused to talk to him, the demons quickly became powerless. It took all her will power to ignore what he was saying rather than argue or defend herself, but it seemed the only way to protect herself. However, the demons were cunning and sometimes caught her off guard.

About this time, the beautiful Light being, Isis, presented herself during one of their channeling sessions. She said she was the Isis of the mythological stories of ancient Egypt, a real person incarnated at that time, but that the myths were greatly exaggerated and distorted through the years, as often happens. She started teaching them about energy flows in detail, among other things. Many of her lessons were primarily for Omaran, to help him understand more about emotional healing.

In one of the conversations they had with Isis, she said, "Omaran, I would like to work with you to help you develop your feminine side more, the nurturing side and the side that can be nurtured; the side that can be receptive and vulnerable. I will help you reawaken this part of you, to bring it into your conscious awareness and make you a more balanced being. You are going through so much! You are asking for and dealing with a tremendous amount of debris and residual from your past."

"Yes, please, I would like any help you can give me," Omaran responded.

"We certainly honor you for this, in fact we push you to go as fast as you can, because the work you are to do is needed. There was a danger for a while that you would not fulfill your agreement, because you put off your healing for so long, and sank into the morass. But we see your intentions now and we are watching very closely." She paused.

Feeling very exposed, he said nothing. This was the first he had heard about having an agreement to do some kind of work, though he understood that most people came into embodiments with missions. He hoped he could fulfill his.

She continued, "Even if you are in the depths of despair, or completely lost in your emotions, you can still call on us and we will try to help you open your heart, to break through the armor that you surround yourself with. It is quite a piece of armor. Very impressive, and built over such a long period of time. You have held it very dear to you.

"Sometimes you do crack it open, and allow your true self out. But there are so many other armors, other shells. One by one is how they are removed—one by one! Just think if you had, say, two hundred shells, or suits of armor. What if you handled one every week, how long would that take? What if you handled one every single day, how long would that take?"

Two hundred shells! That could take a long time! Omaran thought. He said, "There are times when I dig a fairly big hole for myself, and I feel pretty alone and isolated. Intellectually, I'm aware of what I'm doing, but I make it so hard on myself. . . . Your words are very comforting. Why did I create so many suits of armor, so many shells?"

"You have been deeply hurt. How can you wonder why you would put up protection? Everyone does that, not just you. Everyone puts up their own particular kind of protective shell when they are hurt, so they will not be hurt again in that way. In your case, you had a tremendous amount of criticism. A considerable amount in this life, but also some from past lives. And you armored yourself so that you would not have to deal with that.

"But at the same time, all of that criticism went to your heart, and you started to believe all those things that were said to you, that were not true, that were said to hurt. It is very difficult to be criticized thousands of times and not start to believe it. And then your life starts to reflect that. You are now dealing with the impact of it. You now have to reprogram yourself and build your confidence back again—confidence and strength, abilities and talents."

"I want to, I really do. But how?"

"You can recover as you let the shells of armor come off, and fully expose your vulnerability. You don't need to expose it to others, only to yourself, and to your Higher Presence. Every time you take off some armor, you are making yourself vulnerable, opening yourself to attack. Perceived attack. So, your fears will come up. You are acquiring some tools to help you work through these fears and pain, so it can go fast if you use them.

"The development of the nurturing part of you is a very important process right now, so you can feel nurtured and safe while you are going through these vulnerable parts of yourself."

"Thank you, Isis."

"Please tune into the Goddess energy."

Omaran loved to hear these discourses and always resolved to do better, to work harder at his emotional clearing, after listening to the masters. Somehow they made it seem doable to him, at least for a while, though the thought of having two hundred layers to clear was daunting. He had thought he was further along than that!

At least he was beginning to grasp these concepts intellectually, and they made perfect sense. It seemed that he had to sink even lower before it would all be made a part of his experience, however, and stop being merely concepts and words. One of his worst incidents happened on one weekend afternoon in May. Omaran got so angry that he threw Antera's new coffee mug into the kitchen sink in a fit, where it broke into hundreds of pieces and made a startling noise. She watched with horror as his energy expanded, and he looked twice his size. This demon was so inflated that he looked much larger and more powerful than Omaran was, physically. It was frightening, and she was suddenly afraid that he would hurt her, as he pushed out his chest, flexed his muscles, and came for her threateningly. She dodged him, grabbed her keys and purse by the door and ran outside, got in Zippy and drove away. He didn't follow her.

She didn't know where she was going, and they had lived in Mill Valley only six months, so she didn't know her way around the area very well yet. She just knew she had to get away from the monster that was masquerading as her lover. Shaking and taking deep breaths to calm herself, she drove on the freeway for a while and took an exit she had never been on. There was a small shopping center, so she pulled in and parked at the back of the lot, hoping no one would see her. Her face was covered with tears, and she knew her mascara was undoubtedly running.

After closing her eyes for a few moments to try and center herself, she looked outside in front of the car for the first time. There, on top of the roof of a store right in front of her, was a giant inflated gorilla staring down at her menacingly, with arms raised! It reminded her so much of the demon she had just left, that she just stared at it in awe. King Kong! Then she began to laugh. It was just too much, that she had left Omaran's demon to blindly come here and find this now. This had to be a cosmic joke! She laughed out loud almost hysterically, no longer caring whether anyone saw her. Now she knew that she was battling King Kong the giant gorilla, and that is what she would name that demon.

She shouted and sang at the gorilla through her laughter, "Hi Omaran and King Kong up there! You big bully gorilla! Bully, bully, bully!"

The laughter was a good release for her, letting go of the pain and fear. *What an ordeal this is*, she thought. *I'm living with someone who is the perfect match for me, except that he has a demon that resembles King Kong and wants to harm me. Ha! Just a minor glitch in the bliss and happiness between twin flames.* She laughed some more at the ridiculous situation that had engulfed her life.

Feeling much lighter, she mused that this human experience never ceased to amaze her—all the dramas, so real yet so unreal, so easily believed and engaged in. Yet when she had the perspective of the masters, it all looked like a drama on a stage and not reality at all. She mentally gave thanks to her guidance for leading her to that shopping center.

When she got home, she didn't talk to Omaran at all, and he didn't approach her. There was always a silence between them after these rage episodes, sometimes lasting for days. Antera was in a fine mood after her emotional release, but couldn't show that to Omaran, who was feeling remorseful.

Knowing he really did not know how he looked and acted while under the influence of his demons, she thought it may help him to understand. So the next day she remarked in passing, "I saw your biggest demon when I was out yesterday, the one who attacked me—a perfect likeness. You may want to go and check it out."

He didn't know what she was talking about, but that was all she would say about it, just to check it out. She gave him the directions. At his first chance, he did go by there, and saw the giant inflated gorilla on the roof, advertising some kind of store opening. Did he really look like that when he was angry? He thought she must be exaggerating, but he was impressed, and the image stuck in his mind from that time on. It was almost as if by exposing King Kong overtly, he couldn't get away with as much, and he wasn't seen again for a few weeks.

But it wasn't the end of him, unfortunately, and he was back again the next month. He appeared again one evening when they were talking, and when Antera realized it and got up so as not to engage him in talk any longer, he followed her in a threatening way and insisted that she listen to him. She tried to dodge him, but he wanted her to understand just how much he hated her, and she couldn't get away. She was tired of always being the one to leave, and wanted him to leave the house this time, instead. But he wouldn't go, so in desperation, she finally grabbed a smudge stick and started burning sage all around him and the house to clear the energy. She invoked Mother Mary and other masters, praying out loud for protection and help. This infuriated him and his demons even more.

He yelled, "Don't call them, they aren't real anyway! You think those beings are going to help you? Ha! That is stupid. How dare you! Put that sage out!"

But she just kept saying the prayers and walking around with the sage. He came at her and wrestled the sage from her, throwing it on the ground. Then, with a fleeting moment of realization of what he was doing, he turned and left the house, getting into Tan Man and driving off before he could do more damage.

He had no place to go. The truck seemed to drive itself over the familiar roads around town. He didn't want to see anyone, or go to a public place. He was too well known in the area, and sure to see someone he knew. So he simply drove, mostly in circles so as not to get too far away, and finally parked on the road a couple of houses down from their house. He didn't feel well as he slowly came back to present time. As he sat in the darkness alone, watching the occasional car go by and

141

shielding his eyes from the lights, he thought about what had come over him.

Is it true what she says about demons? He wondered. *I'm a good person, how could I have demons, and are there such things? Aren't they part of the darkness, and evil? Maybe I'm not such a good person after all. Maybe I have only been pretending all these years, and fooling everyone, while inside I am very evil. But why, then, do the masters still speak to me through Antera, and why does Antera stay with me if that is true? Oh, God, please help me, I don't know what to do.*

He was suddenly sleepy, and laid down on the truck seat for just a moment, to rest . . . and went into a deep sleep instantly. When he awoke with a start, he turned on the radio to see the clock. It was after 11:00, and he had a sudden strong urge to go home. He knew he would have to face Antera and probably apologize yet again. Maybe she would be asleep and he could sneak in.

When will this end? He wondered. *How can I get control? Is it really me, or is she causing this anger in me?* But he knew that he had had this anger as far back as he could remember, far before he had met Antera. It had always been hard to control, and would come out with no warning. Just when he thought he was getting better, something like this happened. He felt terrible but didn't see a way out.

After he had left, Antera had picked up the sage and finished smudging the house, especially saturating all the corners with the cleansing smoke. She didn't want any of that destructive energy lingering, it was too uncomfortable for her and she knew it would attract more of the same. She sat down on the sofa and cried for half an hour. Maybe it was hopeless, and he would never stop this behavior. The dark side seemed to be winning. Were her guides right about him? Was he really so special that it was worth all this pain to her? She still didn't see a way to help him, and perhaps would never be able to. She wasn't a master, after all, and sometimes felt powerless in the situation.

"What am I expected to do?" She got up and paced, talking out loud to her unseen angel friends. "He isn't getting better, and I'm taking on more and more pain, until pretty soon it may be hopeless that *I* can heal and regain our love even if he *does* get help. Please help me see the reason for this!" She sobbed some more. "I can't keep this up. I'm not as strong as you think I am. He is two people or more, and I only want the part of him that is kind and loving. The rest of him can go to hell. You hear me demons? I DON'T WANT YOU AROUND ANY MORE! GO BACK TO WHERE YOU CAME FROM!"

She closed her eyes and took some deep breaths, and felt better. Sitting down again, she picked up the pen and pad of paper next to her, which she always kept handy, and started writing. The presence of Archangel Metatron was strong, and she could feel that he wanted to communicate something to her. The story that emerged on the paper was about her and Omaran's history together, as seen from the master's perspective. It was as if she were being given a more complete picture of their journey, and how it all fit into what was currently happening. The words flowed out and gave her the understanding she needed to gain perspective on this being she loved. After two hours of writing, she put it down and decided to finish it later.

Closing her eyes, she asked again, more calmly, how she could help this situation.

"Unconditional Love."

The two words flashed across her consciousness, words she had been told many times, and which now took on more significance. Divine love. She started to get it at a deeper level than before. Loving him without any expectations, without taking on his pain, without reacting to his words. Understanding that he was only acting from pain, deep pain, and that what he said had nothing to do with her, absolutely nothing, even though he thought it did when he was angry. Holding the image of him as the radiant Light being he is, and not even acknowledging or listening to the rest. It was just his pain talking, not him. She knew that if she reacted with anger or any emotion at all, it empowered the darkness and pain in him further, and that she needed to be so strong and centered that all the mean things he said went right past her without sticking.

She knew she needed to go beyond her practice of disengaging from him when he was angry, and get to a place within herself where she could love him compassionately at every moment, by understanding the terrible pain he is in. If she could get this mastered, she would truly know Divine Love—the kind of love her guides always had for her, even when she had at times blamed them for things that had not gone right, as if it were their fault, or turned away from them. They loved her no matter what she said or did. This was her big lesson, and she took it on as a worthy challenge.

Suddenly feeling very good, and full of love for Omaran, she closed her eyes and telepathically tuned in to him, to make sure he was all right, and saw a clear image of him in her mind's eye, asleep in the truck, but she couldn't see where. Mentally, she called him and said it was OK to come home now. She sent him a burst of love and felt that it was accepted. Sure enough, ten minutes later, he came through the door. She was still sitting quietly on the sofa, and watched him sheepishly enter, without looking at her. The demons were gone for now, and he looked ashamed for his actions.

He went to the bathroom to get ready for bed, and when he came out she intercepted him in the hallway on the way to the bedroom and hugged him. Love poured into his heart from hers. This took him by surprise, and did so much to ease his suffering that he felt a catch in his throat and almost cried—almost, but he couldn't quite let go.

Her energy flowed and soothed and felt so good that he did not want her to let go. His arms of their own accord went around her, feeling that he didn't deserve it. Something had changed . . . she had never done this before. He let go an involuntary sigh, and after a long moment she released him. He went to bed without a word and she followed shortly after.

His mood improved a bit after that incident. For the next few days after work, Antera worked on finishing the story Metatron had encouraged her to write, and the following weekend she gave it to Omaran to read. "It is a true story except the ending, which I made up because I don't know how it will end yet. I don't know how our relationship will end yet. But I think it may interest you."

She had waited until she knew he was in a good mood, and open. Since the last weekend's big fight, she had been able to keep the love flowing at him, but though she knew her challenge better now, she wasn't sure she could always stay centered while around him. Time would tell. But she knew that the story was written to help him heal.

He looked at the title, *The Twin Flames and the Demons,* and laughed nervously. "I'm not sure I want to read this. . . . " But his curiosity was aroused and he knew he would, right then. "Is it channeled?"

"Yes, I was surrounded by Metatron, who encouraged me to write it. I started it the night you left in anger last weekend, and it has helped me to understand more of what you and I are going through and why." She had no idea what his reaction would be. She left him alone and went into the office, trying to find something to distract her while he read.

Eighteen

The Twin Flames and the Demons

*T*here was once a soul who was given some instruction along his evolutionary path that he thought would help him in his growth back to the Light. This training had become an ingrained part of him, carried from lifetime to lifetime. As one aspect of this training, he was taught to control his emotions, especially his "bad" or "negative" ones, so they would have no influence on his behavior and he could spend all his time in the pursuit of the "higher" emotions and thoughts. He was convinced that this would bring him closer to his God, who was made of only good thoughts and feelings, in contrast to the other God, called the Devil, who contained only bad thoughts and feelings. He thought that if he felt such things as anger or hatred, then he was bringing the Devil into his life and he certainly did not want that.

So he learned to ignore his bad feelings by distracting himself whenever one came up, by putting his mind on something that required his full attention. He thought that made the emotion go away, because he didn't feel it after a while. What he did not know was that every time he took his attention off of those emotions, they didn't really go away. They simply were stored up inside him and carried from lifetime to lifetime until they could be properly expressed. But the system seemed to work well on the surface, and in many lives he was a very pious and well-respected person in his community and church, well rewarded for these efforts. People marveled at how even-tempered he was, and how well he could keep the evil thoughts and feelings from him. Some even thought he was a saint, *and they came to him with their own evil thoughts for help in banishing them.*

After many hundreds of years, he had so effectively suppressed his negative emotions that he no longer even knew what they were, even when one leaked out once in a while, with a force that surprised him and those around him. All those negative emotions were locked up in a box in his heart, sealed off with a lot of energy and intent, so he could maintain his separation between the good and the bad. He trained with the best each society he lived in could give him spiritually, becoming highly adept, but he never addressed the dark Box of Separation, which stored all his pain and was made stronger with each life, requiring more of his energy to keep it intact.

He decided to be born at a time when he could reap the full benefit of accelerated growth around the turn of the millennium 2000, so he could take on all his remaining lessons, which didn't seem too great from his perspective as spirit. This would give him a chance at mastering the Earth existence. He was very advanced spiritually, so if he played his cards right in this lifetime, he would reunite with his Twin Flame and they would ascend together. This was his plan as he came into what he hoped was his final body on Earth.

His Higher Self knew he would have to finally open the Separation Box to heal completely and follow his plans. So he found himself born into a family with a mother who was too sick to care for him, as Spirit presented him with his first healing opportunity: to address his fears and pain of abandonment. His mother, who loved him greatly, had agreed to become sick so she could give this important lesson to him, at the same time providing herself with an opportunity to let go of some of her accumulated karma. But he reacted to the pain in the only way he knew, by ignoring it, and developed a sense of humor that would come out with a joke at just the right time, when feelings of sadness threatened to be expressed.

Even though he was living in a family that did not talk about or support his soul-path to mastery, he knew deep inside that he was more than the body he was in. Sometimes he would lie under the stars at night and wish that a spaceship would come down and take him away. As an old soul surrounded by younger souls, he always felt different in some undefined way, like he didn't really fit in with the society he had been born into. He had an inner need to search for the teachings he needed, so he turned to books as a teenager and found many truths expressed there that felt intuitively right to him, and helped to reawaken his sense of Spirit. It was comforting to find that there were others out there who were different, too, and that there were other ways of thinking than those he had been brought up with. He read about God and Love and Light, and continued his growth in spirit as best he could, considering the great Separation within him. Of course, he didn't consciously know that he carried this burden.

As he grew older, Spirit sent to him the very best teachers, as significant relationships, to help him heal his burden, but he did not have the perspective at the times to realize that. He married and divorced, then remarried, not understanding why problems came up in the relationships. His second wife had lovingly agreed with him in spirit to push him to his limits so he could recognize that he carried the burden. So she said many bad things to him, and criticized him more and more as years went on. He didn't get the message, though, and thought they had lost their love because she was such a bad person. Yet, he stayed with her for many years because he didn't want to leave his children.

The frequent criticisms finally aroused his stored-up anger and frustration of many lifetimes to the point where sometimes the Box leaked and he couldn't stop it. To keep the Box protected, and so he would not have to address it yet, he developed several separate personalities that would respond to the attacks from his wife when they occurred. These sub-personalities took care of the situation each time by fighting back for him. They grew very proficient, finding by trial and error the methods of attack that worked the best, that is, would stimulate the most pain in his wife. She, at the same time, was developing her own sub-personalities. So when they had an argument, their rational selves both left their bodies temporarily, and let these personalities fight. The personalities, which were guarding unexpressed pain, grew very powerful and skilled, and after many years of fighting, when there was no spark of love left between the couple, they finally divorced.

After that "bad" marriage, this man decided he didn't want that to happen again, so he sealed up as best he could the pain in his heart and went into diligent further study of spiritual matters, so he could get away from this planet of pain and suffering. Free of the marriage, he now had more time to meditate and concentrate on his inner work. He was very intuitive in some ways, and began entertaining the notion that there was a woman out there somewhere who was his Soulmate and if he could just find her, he would be whole and all would be well. He called for her often, in his mind.

His Higher Self knew that eventually there would be a showdown between his Light and dark sides, and that the more Light he brought in, the quicker this would happen. There was much concern among his spirit guides that he still had not addressed his stored-up pain, though he had been given many opportunities. Also, the time was drawing near for him to reunite with his Twin Flame and begin their work together. The man's calls for her were speeding that process. Would he be ready in time, or would the meeting be premature, before he was healed enough to handle the intensity of such a relationship?

His Twin Flame was a woman who had also chosen to be born at this time of spiritual acceleration. She was born into a large family of old souls and had much spiritual support growing up, but soon found that she was very different from most people in the outside world. She was very energy-sensitive, which made her quiet and shy in a world of people who didn't sense what she did, and no one taught her how to hold her own energy intact so she could differentiate between hers and others' feelings.

She knew from an early age, by contact with her spirit guides, that she had an important mission in this life, but that her real work wouldn't start until the end of the century approached and she was over forty. As a teenager, the woman wrote poetry that entertained the notion of having a very special partner who walked in the woods and shared deep spiritual intimacies with her. She thought she would know this person if they met, but gradually gave up on finding him. She followed her urge to have children while very young, so they would be grown by the time her real work started.

With her first husband, she studied the physical body and reviewed her mastery of it. She gave birth to two sons, and studied nutrition and health. She never thought this husband was one she would stay with her whole life, but she knew they had this work to do together, and when it was done, they moved apart. With her second husband, she reviewed the emotional body. The two of them, as their Higher Selves, had arranged to push each other to get in contact with the unexpressed rage they both had inside. They had energetic verbal fights, which prompted her to dive into some intense work to release lifetimes of pain. She studied the ways of the emotional body while she healed and cleared her own emotional flow. With that lesson reviewed, the marriage had served its purpose and they split.

Her third husband was a scientist like herself, and with him she studied and re-mastered the mental body, developing her left-brain knowledge and logic as well as discharging subconscious mental patterns that no longer served her. She didn't believe that this husband was her True Mate any more than the other two were, but it was a happy marriage, and she was content. However, a part of her deeply wanted to be able to share her spiritual journey with her mate, which she couldn't do. So she turned to her personal connection with beings of Light, and her personal support group in spirit who continued to teach her and illumine her path.

The agreed-upon time came, and (with some hesitation) the Higher Selves of the man and woman cunningly arranged for them to be in the same place at the same time, on several occasions. When they met, it was not instantaneous recognition, but after a few brief conversations they hugged and both felt a vast expansion of Divine Love, and they knew within a short period of time that they were meant to be together. There was an attraction that was far greater than they had felt with anyone else, because it was of so many dimensions. They quickly realized that they shared the same spiritual goals along similar paths, and it was deeply satisfying to share this part of their lives together, which neither had been able to do with previous spouses.

At first, the man thought his dream of finding the right mate had come true, because they had so much fun together and they connected at such deep levels, and this was refreshing after the fighting in his previous marriage. But he became frightened when the newness of their sacred union wore off and little things started to upset him. The woman could read his energy, so when the man got upset she would ask what he was upset about. The woman thought that all upsets should be dealt with as soon as they come up, between two people in an intimate relationship.

But his old training made him deny being upset because he thought such things weren't felt by spiritual beings, especially men.

As their sacred union accelerated their spiritual work together and the Light started seeping into little corners of the Separation Box inside the man's heart, the sub-personalities he had created in his previous marriage started to reappear. These personalities thought that the Light was their mortal enemy, a very reasonable thought since the Light was starting to penetrate the Box they guarded and it was threatening their security. They also thought that any woman in the man's life was an enemy.

So the man started to let these personalities energetically and verbally attack the woman. She was not at all prepared for the onslaught and was deeply hurt by what he said. He even said he thought they should not be together, which broke her heart. The personalities knew that if they could convince her of that, their Box would be safe.

After this sort of thing happened several times, the woman started to notice that every time the man got mad or frustrated, he would say the same things, and she started to call the personalities he gave his power to "demons." She gradually accepted that these demons weren't the man she was in love with, and this was a relief to her. But when the woman explained all this to the man, hoping he would then get some help in exorcising the demons, it was to no avail. She told him that all she wanted from him was love, and if he wanted to hold onto all that suppressed energy and put off his healing that was OK as long as he didn't allow the demons to take out their energy on her. He agreed that love was a reasonable request, and at first he tried to make agreements about how he would behave when he felt angry, but he couldn't keep them because he couldn't hold the demons to those agreements. In fact, he couldn't control the demons at all. When these agreements were broken, his mate started to think that maybe there was no hope for the relationship to work.

With time, the man gradually did come to agree that he had some difficulties with his emotional body, though he did not admit this to his mate. So he prayed and asked for help at taking the pain away, in a most convincing way. He understood quite rightly that whenever you asked your Higher Self and spirit guides for help, it was given. The man thought that the angels and masters could just reach into his energy and take all those lower emotions away, doing the hard work for him, so he wouldn't have to go through all that pain. What he didn't understand was that they couldn't take it away without his releasing it physically as well. They helped him break down the walls of his Separation Box even more quickly because of his requests, in the hopes that he would find a way to release all that would be exposed.

This was accomplished very cleverly by arranging meetings for him on the inner planes, mostly while he was sleeping so he did not remember them. Each meeting was to set up an agreement with various people who would help him bring these emotional energies up so they could be recognized and addressed, and then (hopefully) healed. The work was designed to help the other people involved, as well, by releasing some kind of karmic debt in exchange for helping him.

As the agreements manifested in the man's physical reality, one by one and sometimes all at once, fears were brought to his attention by the playing out of dramas in all areas of his life. The dramas were very real and painful for him, and it seemed that whatever he feared, happened. He understood on an intellectual level the concept of creating your own reality, but he hadn't accepted this truth in his experience. So it appeared to him that the more he asked for help, the worse things became. His Higher Self was patiently waiting for the man to realize that he had to release the emotions that were being brought up, but he continued to hold on by sheer force of his will, which was very strong indeed.

As his fears grew, however, his protective demons grew even more powerful than his will, and they took control of his behavior more and more often. The man had enough control to keep them buried most of the time when he and the woman were in the company of friends, but he couldn't control them when he was alone with his mate, and she was often verbally attacked. The woman could see what was happening and tried very hard not to be hurt by what the demons said, but she wasn't always successful.

When the man was fully present, she taught him what she knew about emotional release. He would listen and accept what she said, but still couldn't control the demons, who, naturally, did not want him to get help. All the suggestions she made were promptly forgotten. He also had the notion that to ask for help would be the equivalent of admitting that he was wrong, and that he wasn't really as advanced along his spiritual path as everyone else thought. The demons fully supported his inaction.

His mate had almost lost hope that he would win the battle between his Light and dark sides. She knew that she needed to love him, and that if she could do that all the time, it would help him heal. She needed to rally her forces to become the most perfect expression of Divine Love, because this kind of Love was a force that nothing could fight against, and the solution to any problem. This was her big lesson. She asked her guides to help open her heart, taking in all the Love she could possibly hold, and then transmitted it to her mate daily. As the woman practiced her expression of Divine Love, she saw a definite shift in the amount of time the demons were in charge. But if she slacked off in her focus, the demons almost immediately took over again.

The happy part of this story is the made-up ending, because it hasn't happened yet: The man eventually began starting the process of healing and release. It finally came to him that if he ignored the help that was offered, he may not ever get out of the morass. He also realized that his True Love was with him to help him heal, and she was not the enemy. If he didn't accept that, his chance at such a perfect union and world service would be lost, as well as his chance to achieve mastery in this lifetime. There was too much at stake for him to be letting the demons control him anymore. He accepted help from his mate and worked diligently on release of his pain from his childhood and many past lifetimes.

So in the end, despite all the suffering, Divine Love and Light won the battle and the Sacred Union of Twin Flames was preserved. They went on to be great teachers of the Light, inspiring others to overcome their blockages, and ascended together into the bliss of Higher Presence. . . .

Omaran wept several times while reading the story. He couldn't hold the tears back, and didn't even try. It rang so true, and for the first time he really started to see how his behavior was seen from the masters' perspective. He felt terrible about how he had hurt his mate so. The small trickle of tears cleansed him, and he felt purified. He read it twice through.

"Antera?"

She came back in to the living room and sat across from him. "How did you like it?" She could see that he was touched.

"It's wonderful. I really didn't know . . . I am so sorry, I had no idea that it hurt you so much. Thank you, this is a gift—and the truth." He straightened his posture. "But I still don't like the idea of 'demons.' I don't like you calling them that . . ." But it was said with a light heart.

The story had a very healing effect on Omaran, and he thought about it for days, reading parts of it again. The demons had been overtly exposed. He felt such relief, as if now his whole body could relax. A deep place inside, where he didn't even know he had been holding tension, had simply let go. Now he knew how good it felt after crying, even that little bit, and wished he could do it more often, as Antera had suggested so many times. But why was it so hard?

No wonder she calls them demons, he thought. *I can't control them . . . they have power over me. I can't will them away!* Frightened for a moment, he wondered if he could ever gain control over them. He had accomplished so many things in his life by using his will; he had always been able to make things happen. But his will alone was no match for these demons, or the problem would be already taken care of. How did he will something not to happen? *Wait! These demons are not beings separate from me, controlling me from the outside. They are my own creation, they are parts of myself—so of course I can and will conquer them!*

This resolve resulted in improved behavior for a few months. He was happier and kinder than he had been in a while. But Antera was wary. Though she enjoyed their times together, she knew the demons would be back because most of the repressed energy was still there, and she knew it would take a lot of work to clear. So she kept her guard up. It was just too easy to forget the bad times when he was his joyful self.

Nineteen

Now,
we bear the Light,
a million flames
burning bright,
connecting hearts
around the world.
Together we shine
like never before.
Together.

— From the song
"Now (Lightworkers' Anthem)"

Antera's guidance had been urging her for several years to quit her scientific work so she could go into more satisfying and creative work. She had loved the challenge of science at first, but now she didn't enjoy it as much. Some memories of previous lives, when she had been a scientist and loved the joy of research and discovery, had been a strong influence in her decision to go in that direction in this lifetime. Her thirst for mental stimulation had led her into physics and math, then her love of the Earth had brought her finally to geophysics and seismology.

Earthquakes had always fascinated her, with their immense power and unpredictability, an interest sparked by memories of being in some massive seismic events in past lives. There was something about earthquakes that literally shook people to their very foundations, much more than other potentially disastrous events from nature. She thought this was because people depended so much on the stability of the Earth beneath them, without really realizing it until it shook. The process of how and why earthquakes happen drew her attention still, especially the possibility of predicting them, and if she could have done pure research, she probably wouldn't think of leaving the field.

But the days of governmental funding of research were over, and now there was a lot of competition for the moneys. This kind of competition among scientists was not healthy, being a field that depended on cooperation and sharing of ideas—it tended to corrupt the whole scientific process.

That was why she worked as an engineering seismologist in the small consulting company, mathematically predicting the ground motions at particular sites of future potential earthquakes, mostly for the retrofitting of dams, bridges, and other important structures. It required cranking through the same processes and computer programs again and again, and she felt her large flow of creative energy being stifled. Though she was good at it, it required so much of her time and energy that it was increasingly hard to stay focused on it as her interests evolved in other areas.

Going to part-time wasn't an option because of the intensity and pressure to stay on top of the literature and publish. It required a good sixty-hour workweek to maintain the career, and though that had seemed like a vacation after the hard work of graduate school at University of California at Berkeley, it was too much now that her interest had waned.

She argued with her guides when they suggested she could find other work. After all, she still owed $40,000 for her education, with big loan payments every month. But she knew it would happen, it was only a matter of time. She also knew that the longer she waited, and ignored what Spirit was telling her, the more likely she would create an uncomfortable situation in which she would have to leave. She had gone through that before, by not responding to the urgings of the universal flow. But what could she do to take its place financially? Teach meditation, channeling, or metaphysics? She didn't think that would pay the bills.

She had discussed this with Omaran many times, and no solutions had presented themselves. But one day in early July, he declared, "You know? It just came to me that I can support both of us while you change careers, for a year or so anyway. My construction business is going strong, and I have two big remodels lined up, so I don't see any reason you can't quit your job right away."

Antera was amazed, and truly touched. None of her previous husbands had supported her, so it had never occurred to her that Omaran, to whom she was not even married, would or could do that. She had always had to work, since she was very young, putting herself through undergraduate and graduate school, while raising two children. It had not been an easy path.

"Really? You would do that?"

"Of course. It would be great to have you freed up to do more teaching and put more effort into creating the spiritual center. That would benefit both of us." He was feeling better and better about this decision; it really felt right.

So she immediately gave four weeks' notice at her job, and a month later she was free. Her home office became the place she nested, and she was able to devote more time to classes, writing, and other projects. It was very fulfilling, though tight financially. The projects she and Omaran did together were joyful—provided they only discussed them when he was lucid.

Their friends and students never saw his dark side, and he was well respected as a spiritual teacher. He played the part well, and others only saw his heart as open and loving. And to them he was. Sometimes Antera inwardly blanched when people praised him for being so clear and loving, knowing how he was sometimes, but she did recognize the wonderful spiritual gifts he honestly shared with groups.

Antera put together a number of other courses and brought in other teachers as well, as the work expanded through the rest of the year. She created the spiritual center as a nonprofit corporation, handling all the legal paperwork herself. They built a stone circle in their back yard and held their full-moon ceremonies there each month through the spring, summer and fall, moving indoors when the winter rains came. The weekly meditations in their living room, which they had also resumed when they got their house in Mill Valley, grew in size all year as people told their friends.

Michael had continued to attend all their weekly meditations, blossoming in his spiritual growth, and now knew how to manage his energy broadcasting abilities to such an extent that he was one of the best transmitters of healing energy they knew. At the end of each channeled meditation, participants had the option of going into the center of the circle, stating a problem they wanted energy for, and receiving healing energies from the group. This was where he excelled.

He had remained a very good friend of theirs. Their shared experiences and memories enriched their connection and strengthened their bond. The three of them had learned a great deal through it all, and increased their faith tremendously. The unseen guides, who had strongly advised them through what could have been disastrous times, had helped to create an incredibly smooth transition, and they felt very fortunate to have shared it, despite the difficulties.

Michael adored Omaran and learned a lot about living a spiritual life from him. Omaran felt that Michael had the most open heart of anyone he had ever met, and this continued to touch him deeply. Antera was very thankful that it had turned out so well, and loved Michael as a soul brother.

On one of the weekly mediation evenings in September, Michael brought a new friend. He introduced her as Linda, and there were sparks of energy between them. She was a devotee of Sri Ramakrishna, but open to seeing what Michael liked so much about these gatherings. And she really wanted to meet the two people he was so close to, especially Antera, his ex-wife. Linda sat with the group without participating fully, but instead doing her own meditation process. After the others left, Michael and Linda stayed to talk.

"So when did you two meet?" Omaran asked enthusiastically as the four of them settled after all the goodbye hugs.

"Oh, a few weeks ago in a store, actually," said Michael. "We just clicked right away, and we've been seeing each other often since. Linda lives very close to me in Berkeley, and we take BART to the city in the morning together. And the funny thing is, we work in buildings just a few blocks apart in San Francisco, as well. So we meet for lunch, too." He looked at Linda and they smiled at each other.

"Ah, so what do you do in San Francisco, Linda?" Omaran asked.

She explained about the nonprofit organization she worked for, and her daughter in high school, and they talked for another half an hour. Linda had a delightful way with words and kept it light and humorous when conversation turned to Michael's many ex-wives. Before long, Michael said they had to get up early and they left.

Michael called the next evening. "Well, what do you two think of Linda?"

Antera had answered the phone. "She's very nice. But you certainly don't need our approval."

"No, but I like to get your impressions and thoughts. We are practically living together now. I'm keeping my apartment because there is no room at hers for my stuff, but I'm over there most of the time. So do you like her?"

"Well, yes, though I hardly talked with her. The important thing is, does she make you happy? Do you have fun together? Do you love her?"

"Yes to all. We seem to be very compatible. I think she's good for me."

"Well, then. We are very happy you've found someone to be with." She really was happy for him. It had been such a difficult few years for him, starting with her leaving him, then Patti's death almost two years ago, and no one since. She hoped this new relationship would work. "How did she like the meditation and the group, anyway?"

"She thought it was OK, but she has her own spiritual practice. I think she is willing to attend just because I like it. What you guys do doesn't interfere with what she believes, so she just kind-of merges the two and it works for her." Michael was really glad of that. It was very important to him that they could share spiritual experiences. If she would go along, it was a big plus.

So Linda became a regular at the meetings through the winter, at first acting very guarded and not sharing anything with the group. But gradually she understood that Antera and Omaran didn't have any agenda of wanting devotees or followers, as they respected the range of beliefs held by members of the group. Over the next few months, Linda started opening up and sharing experiences with the others, in a way that was entertaining and inspiring. She was a good addition to the group as her heart opened.

After a dinner at their home celebrating the Winter Solstice, she sent a nice thank-you note that said: "The food was all so sumptuous and the people . . . ah, the people. Where else can I go and 'party' with warm, loving, self-revealing people who routinely commune with Jesus, Mary, Archangels, spirit guides, et al., AND, who regard this as perfectly normal??!!!"

They got a good laugh out of that.

The following February, Michael and Linda announced that they were engaged. They were married on the Spring Equinox, with Omaran and Antera leading part of the ceremony. It was a small, unusual gathering, attended by the bride's ex-husband and his lady, and the groom's ex-wife (Antera) and her man—plus a couple of their kids and the minister. At the very moment they finished their vows, standing in a medicine wheel on Mt. Tamalpais under a large oak, a loud horn blew from far down on the beach below, and they all laughed and hooted. It seemed like a very fitting send-off to their marriage, and the timing was perfect.

Antera was very happy for Michael, but his remarriage did send her thoughts back to the marriage issue between her and Omaran. They had been together much longer than Michael and Linda, over three years now. She had tried not to think about it over that time—it had been so painful at first that she thought she would never heal the broken heart. Sometimes she was glad they hadn't tied the knot, because she wasn't sure they would be together for long. Being twin flames just didn't seem to be enough. Perhaps Omaran had known at a deep level about his emotional damage, and that had kept him from committing. It was for the best now, anyway. They could just take their relationship one day at a time, like they had been doing. "Will we be together today or not?" That was her daily question.

"So what's the deal, anyway? Why don't you have work?" Antera asked Omaran as they finished lunch at home, sitting at their small dining table.

It was late March, a week after Michael and Linda's wedding, and she glanced out at the apple trees in the back yard, nestled between the tall redwoods. Their small bright green leaves were full of new life, and the recently-dropped blossoms covered the ground like snow. She loved staying home to work among the trees, but their money situation was now critical, because Omaran's construction work had tapered off with the approach of winter, and now, months later, no recovery was in sight.

He answered, "I don't know. I'm just not getting any calls. Normally it picks up by now, as the rain starts tapering off and people think about remodeling projects."

"Well, isn't there anything you can do? We can't keep borrowing money to live on, and the teaching and other spiritual projects sure don't pay the bills, especially the college costs for our kids. There must be some way for you to bring in work." She definitely thought he should be doing more than he appeared to be doing.

"I think it is just the economy. When it is low people don't hire contractors." He shrugged. "I don't know what I can do about it."

"Well, surely you can use energy work to magnetize customers to you. We have been given some great tools from the masters. How about using them for this? I don't believe this is about the economy. You are responsible for whatever happens in your work, because we all create our lives as they are. Don't you believe this? Do you think you are powerless here?"

"I know the masters have told us that, but those are just words to me. I don't really know what to do, how to use the tools. I don't know how to change the economy or the weather. I don't have control of those things. It isn't that simple!" Omaran didn't like the direction this conversation was going. There was no way he was going to take responsibility for his lack of work; it was beyond his control and that was that.

"Until you take some time alone to meditate on it and figure out just why this is happening, and I mean the deeper reasons behind it, and work on changing whatever is getting in the way of money flow, nothing will change. Remember, you promised you would support us when I quit my job."

"I don't know how to just 'magnetize customers.' I know it isn't a good situation, but stop getting on my case about it." He got up from the table and walked out the front door, and into the small garage in the driveway. He sat down on a bench and stared at his vast collection of carpentry tools.

Do I really have to take responsibility for not having work? He thought about the work he had been doing for so many years. After he had finished his college degree in music, then co-written and co-starred in an off-Broadway musical in New York back in the late 60s, he had thought he'd be performing and writing music for a living. After the show ended and the group broke up, he had tried to keep his music career going. But after living in both Los Angeles and New York, he had known that if living in a big city was required, he would have to find something else. The big cities seemed to drain off his energy, and he wanted to be able to choose where he lived.

Giving up his music career had not been easy, and he had always thought he'd get back to it at some time in his life. Once he had made the decision, though, he began reading a lot, and after a while found that he was drawn to books on architecture by Buckminster Fuller and Frank Lloyd Wright. Back in college, he had been an engineering student before switching to music, so he had some previous experience in drafting and design. The idea of designing and building houses had grown quickly in his mind, so he had enrolled in a drafting course again, and also became a carpenter's apprentice, so he could do both. It seemed like the ideal new career.

He reflected on those early days of his new work. How he had loved the building process! It was such a gift, to be outdoors most of the time, and to be a part of the magic of materializing finished dwellings out of empty space! And best of all, he could do it anywhere, and live anywhere he wanted! Though he had intended for this construction career to be temporary, he had soon found himself locked in, with a family to support. He had built some really beautiful custom homes in Marin County in the last couple of decades.

But thinking about building suddenly made him feel very heavy and tired. Standing up to shake the feeling off, he realized that he really didn't want to do construction work anymore. He had lost interest in it years ago. There was so much more joy in doing the projects he and his mate were doing together, and he felt like they were really doing their highest service there. Plus, he was getting up there in years, and though his body was in great shape, he could feel it slowing down just a bit. He would never admit it to anyone, but he knew he wasn't quite as strong as he used to be.

Pacing back and forth in the tiny space around his tools, he wondered if this was the "deeper reason" Antera had been bugging him about. In the back of his mind, he had been hoping all along that the spiritual work would take off quickly and make enough money to support them so he wouldn't have to do this construction anymore.

He also knew that his fears of lack had been stimulated in a big way, and that this probably contributed to his inability to get out and find the work he needed. He was afraid that he may not be able to pay for his children's college costs, which would alienate them even more, not to mention that he and Antera might lose the house and all they possessed.

But what to do about it, that was the question. Praying was the only thing he could think of right now, so he continued that, hoping that the universe would provide other sources of income besides construction. On his own, he couldn't think of any other practical skills he had that could make enough money to support them.

The financial situation slowly built up frustration in Antera. She took time one day when she had a few hours alone to vent her anger by pacing and shouting at the universe and her spirit guides. Her guides had clearly said that she would be "provided for" if she quit her job. So what was happening? Where was the flow? Why didn't Omaran have work? Was she being dragged into Omaran's financial difficulties?

"How do you expect me to have faith in my guidance after trusting what you said about being provided for in my career change, only to find that it didn't happen? Did I misunderstand you? Was there a major change? Do I have to get another job now, and tell me, how can it be the highest path for me to go back to work? It will only mean that I'll have to stop teaching and creating the spiritual center! There won't be time! How can this be best? Grrrr!"

She took some deep breaths and blew out forcefully, shaking her body all over and letting the frustration go. "OK, I know it isn't my guides' fault, and that I'll learn in time why this is happening, but that doesn't make it easier to go through now! Please help me understand!"

Her guides just listened, and let her release her frustration first. When she had calmed down and was sitting quietly, they then showed her pictures from a past life that was pivotal in relation to this situation.

In that lifetime, as now, she had blamed her guidance for leading her into some bad times, much worse than she was in now. She had made agreements before that lifetime that clearly spelled out her life path, but when she was then incarnated and the planned events occurred, she thought she had been led astray. It was time to understand that what she had gone through in that lifetime had helped humanity and inspired others' faith, and therefore it was worth the suffering. The pain from that time was still with her, and had been triggered by the current situation so it could be healed.

She cried for a while, and worked more on releasing her pain from that past time, which was very real to her. It became clear that her faith was being tested, and she finally understood a basic concept: that having faith while things are going well is easy, but it is when things don't go the way we want, that we really build faith. She came away with a renewed trust in the Higher Plan, accepting once again that it didn't always go where she consciously thought it should, but that in the end, the highest good would be served, as it always was. It was just part of being incarnated as a human that she couldn't always see the final outcome, and that is why it helped to trust in the God-force, which has a much greater, far-reaching plan.

After Antera had worked through her resistance and accepted the fact that she had to get outside work, she started her search. Being trained in science, in such a specialized field, made it a bit difficult to transfer skills to another profession, but she knew she had a lot of skills and it would be a matter of convincing an employer of that. She modified her resume so she didn't appear to be overqualified for everything.

Her guidance told her that a perfect situation would present itself and it would be effortless, so instead of looking at classified ads, she first put out some feelers, emailing a few friends and letting them know that she was looking for work. One such email went to Byron, a man she and Omaran had met through a mutual friend. Byron owned a small publishing firm that specialized in spiritual books. They both liked him, a kind man in his forties, with a strong work ethic driven by wanting to make a difference in the world. He called her the next day.

"We could sure use some help around here, someone who can do a little of everything, assisting me and the production manager. I can't pay much, but I'd sure appreciate it if you would help us out for a couple of weeks anyway."

It sounded like secretarial work to her, and she didn't have typing or other skills along those lines. "Oh, I don't think so. I need something that pays more and is more permanent. But please let me know if anything else comes up that you may be able to use me for, or if you hear of anything. I'd really appreciate it."

"OK, well let me know if you change your mind. We'd love to have you here. Say hi to Omaran for me."

After she hung up, she got the distinct feeling that her guidance wanted to tell her something. She sat quietly, closed her eyes and listened. She heard, "Are you sure you want to turn that down? Perhaps you want to reconsider."

She protested, "But it is part time, only for a couple of weeks, and not a kind of work I do well."

"You never know what an opportunity like this might turn into later. . . ."

She said she'd consider it and mulled the thought over for the rest of the day. At least she didn't have to give Byron a resume, because he knew her, and her guides seemed to think there would be something else coming of it, perhaps another connection. Well, she could certainly do two weeks and it wouldn't be that bad. She called Byron back the next morning.

"I've reconsidered, and would be happy to come help you out for a couple of weeks. When do you want me to start?"

He was pleased. "How about tomorrow, 9:00?"

"Sounds fine."

"You'll be working with the production manager. I'm sure you will like her."

She did like her a lot. It was satisfying to work with Byron in his small spirit-based company. The work was easy, and helped pay the bills. When two weeks were up, she was asked to stay a few weeks longer and agreed, and when those weeks were gone, she was still there. They gave her more and more responsibility and the work turned into full-time management within half a year. She was out in the world again, making money and also learning some new skills. And she was very thankful that her guidance had encouraged her to take the job, such as it was in the beginning.

Twenty

Barriers around us,
darkness that we held,
all the resistance
and fears are now dispelled.
Confronted by the Light,
they vanish easily.
Now our path ahead
is clear and free.
We shall lead, we shall lead.

— From the song
"Now (Lightworkers' Anthem)"

The rest of their fourth year together went by fast, because, coincidentally enough, shortly after Antera started working, Omaran found full-time work as well. They had to cut way back on their teaching and other activities, but they did continue doing energy work with the geometrical forms, and this was making both of them more energy sensitive. More and more they were noticing how energy moved through their bodies differently each day. Sometimes it was strong, like a large river, other times it was very subtle.

Isis, who had been their primary teacher on flows of energy, had explained that these flows were due to several variables. First, a human being's ability to receive varied a lot, depending on their emotional, mental and physical condition. Second, the immediate environment influenced the flow because of the psychic energy of others around them, past and present. And third, the overall energies of the planet fluctuated because of the cosmic energies coming in, and also because of the inherent energies due to mass thought-forms and feelings.

In late August, they both noticed that the energy flow through their bodies was very large, gushing in and through. It seemed significant, so they asked their guidance if there was anything going on cosmically.

Archangel Metatron came through with a message: "There have been some changes in the last few days, major shifts, based on decisions that have been made by the spiritual Hierarchy and by the greater Hierarchy of the Galaxy. As these changes go into effect there could be some major chaos occurring within certain regions on the planet. We will not be able, much longer, to hold back the flood of new energies that approach the planet. We have been filtering them to protect humanity from a sudden influx, keeping the rise in frequency at a rate that can be integrated into all of your bodies. But this large wave that has just been released in the last few days was allowed, to see what happens—as a test of the spiritual climate on the planet."

"We can feel it, like our energy is very expanded the last few days. Do you advise that we do something special?" Omaran asked him.

"If you could spend all day in meditation for the next few days, I would recommend it. For keeping tuned to these changes is essential for your own rapid growth. To adjust your bodies to the new frequencies, you must realign by holding your focus and getting your direction from the highest source."

"OK, we will. Is everyone else affected by this rush of energy?"

"Most of it is being focused or funneled into the light bearers like yourselves, so they can help in its integration. You are being asked to take on a higher voltage of energy so you can directly confront dark forces of the past and present, bringing more Light to the planet."

After receiving that information, they decided to take the next three days off. Fortuitously, Omaran had just finished a job so he could take the time, and Antera's schedule was flexible. He intuitively knew the perfect spot on Mt. Tamalpais, overlooking the ocean and surrounded by majestic bay trees. They spent the three days there while fasting on fruit juice, to help their bodies remain pure, and went home each night.

Most of the time was spent in silent meditation, with their eyes either open and looking at the view or closed, while they perceived the large flow of energy. They asked for guidance and direction, and how to best use this flow. The days went by amazingly fast, as they got into a zone where time was no longer perceived as strongly.

On the third day, a radiant being suddenly appeared to Antera, someone she had not met before, and he appeared so bright that she tried to shield her eyes, but realized that they were already closed. He said he was to be the Guardian and Initiator of the large pyramid temple that would be built for the spiritual center they were planning. He felt like an old friend, and she telepathically talked with him for quite a while, learning more about the initiations in the pyramid temples of ancient Egypt. Back in those days, he said, he was an initiator in the pyramid temple where she was trained and initiated, prior to becoming a teacher herself.

"Was I initiated in the Great Pyramid? Did I finish my training there?" She had been wondering about that, and had fragmented memories of being there.

"Yes, you did go through all seven initiations at that time, and emerged as a fully realized being."

"You mean I was enlightened?"

"Yes."

"Then why am I still here? Did I do something terribly bad that made me have to come back? What happened?" She had often thought she must be one of the slowest learners on the planet, still here after so many thousands of years.

He answered, "At that time you were freed of the need to incarnate any more. But when you were given the choice to move on or to stay here and help others reach that state, you chose to come back for another set of incarnations."

"Why on Earth would I do that?"

"Because of your great compassion and love for humanity. It was by your choice that you returned, not by mistake or karma or your own need."

She had to let this sink in for a few moments. Then she said, "I have always been embarrassed about being here so long, especially because I feel I have already experienced all this planet has to offer. Now you are telling me I chose to stay here?"

"Exactly. You chose to take on more of the darkness and transform it, just because you COULD. Since then you have been serving in many different ways, sometimes choosing very difficult paths."

". . . So what about Omaran?"

"He made the same choice."

"Are there others?"

"Oh, yes."

She thanked him for his visit. She was incredibly relieved to find this out about her soul journey. It resonated as truth to her, and it solved a conundrum she had puzzled over for years. Her entire outlook was changed permanently, and she felt very blessed.

Afterwards, she told Omaran all that she could remember. He thought it very interesting. Though he had no memories of the times in ancient Egypt, it felt like truth to him as well.

Antera added, "Did you know that we will be building a large pyramid for the center we are planning?"

He noted the new sparkle in her eyes. "Wow, that would be amazing. Actually, the thought has crossed my mind."

"It will be strictly for initiations and meditations, not for just anyone to use," she clarified.

"Right. . . ." He was already picturing it in his mind, as the builder he was. What would it be made of? How big? It was exciting to see how their mission together unfolded, one piece at a time.

They went home that evening knowing that the new cosmic energy flow was on the wane, and they had ridden it out successfully. It had been a good experience. They broke their fast with a salad and went to bed early.

The next morning, Antera had a stomachache, which was unusual, but she dismissed it as an after-effect of the fast. She was sitting on the couch doing her morning meditation after Omaran left for work, when a sudden rush of tremendous Light flowed into her system. She sat with it for a while, feeling as though she was being "pumped up" by her guides to yet a new level of flow. She directed the energy to permeate all her cells and awaken them, letting go of any resistance they had to the Light.

As soon as the energy flow started abating, the phone rang and it was her sister Janet. She told Antera that she was very concerned about a mutual friend who had joined a religious cult. The friend believed that the leader was God, or Jesus reincarnated, and had seemingly given him all her power, allowing him to completely control her life. Janet had learned that the leader had even physically abused the friend, kicking her and breaking a rib, but the friend thought it was all right, and that she had deserved it.

"I'm really concerned about her. Would you please check in with your guidance about it?" Janet asked. "I'm wondering if there is anything I can do."

"OK, I'll call you back in an hour or so."

As she sat down to connect with her guidance, suddenly the pain in Antera's stomach got worse, and she felt a coldness descend over her, causing her to start shaking. She realized that a powerful force was trying to interfere with her connection—and she knew in the next instant that it was the being associated with the cult leader, the one who was "overshadowing" the leader. This being wanted to communicate with her. She also intuitively knew that the surge of Light that had been pumped into her before the phone call had been her angels' way of getting her ready for this encounter with a dark lord, which was exactly how he appeared to her.

Just then, Omaran walked through the door unexpectedly, saying he had forgotten something for work. She was glad to see him, told him what was happening and he sat down with her to support her energetically. She gathered her strength and faced the vast darkness, describing to Omaran what was going on as it happened.

The dark being was presenting himself in a very frightening way, huge and powerful. She couldn't see his face, just his form and the energy radiating from him. She held her energy steady, concentrating on feeling like a Pillar of Light.

She confronted him directly. "Who are you?"

He shook his head and wouldn't say his name.

"What do you want?"

"To bring you to my side, so we can be allies. I can teach you to use your power more effectively. See how much power I wield!"

There was intense turmoil in her solar plexus, and in a flash she knew that this encounter was the reason for her stomach pain. She held firm to the Light, feeling his power, but not being scared of it, knowing that he could do no harm to her. In fact, it seemed that her own Light power was growing to match his. "What makes you think I would want to be your ally?"

"Because you used to be aligned with us and can come back. It is not too late. Try to remember!"

"If I have ever been aligned with the dark side, which I don't remember, it doesn't matter because now I am fully aligned with the Light. Any mistakes I've made have been forgiven completely."

He tried another tack. "Duality is simply an illusion, don't you agree?"

"Yes, I agree."

"So then it really doesn't matter which side you are on, one is not better than the other. They are simply two sides to the same coin. Why not be on the side that can give you fame and power to influence people and do great things on the planet? I can guarantee that!"

She said nothing. He leaned closer. "We could do great things together, you and I. Work with me and I can help you get what you want much quicker, even the spiritual center you want to create."

"I am aligned with the Light." She repeated this several times, as he tried various ways to convince her that his way was better. The pain in her stomach was still great, as if he was trying to tap her energy at the solar plexus and she was resisting. Then she decided that she had put up with enough and told him, "Look, if you want to heal you can do so, partially or fully, right now. Perhaps I can help you."

She deliberately moved the sphere of energy at her stomach slowly upward to her heart, and opened her heart wide, pouring out a large flow of love and compassion toward him. She found that she sincerely loved him, and wanted him to know it.

She mentally told him, "Here, take this Love, and do anything you want with it."

The gesture completely surprised him, catching him off guard. "I don't want it!" And he gathered the energy and returned it to her . . . then it hit him, what he had done. He had sent love energy to her! This visibly unnerved him—he suddenly knew he had made a terrible mistake.

"You tricked me!" he shouted, as his energy weakened, dissipated, and he quickly slunk away without another word.

She was surprised at his reaction. She hadn't intended to trick him, but apparently had intuitively done the right thing. Immediately, her stomach felt fine. She contacted her guidance without interference. They were all there, and a lot of activity was going on in the inner planes. She was congratulated, and told more of the history of the being she had confronted.

There was a long history of this being on the planet, and the cult leader was one of the people who were currently in his service. The leader was highly psychic, and the dark lord had convinced him that he was very special, very powerful, appealing to his ego. His abilities impressed the people who followed him.

Antera's guidance said, "This has been a problem with many of the 'spiritual' leaders on the planet through the ages. People tend to think that anyone who has some psychic abilities and can see into realms they can't, or sense the future, or tell them things about themselves that they couldn't have known, are spiritually advanced. That is why they follow them, thinking that they are the way to God. But it is not so. The process of developing psychic senses is fairly independent of the evolution of the soul. In fact, some of the most highly evolved beings incarnated now are not strongly psychic, and deliberately chose not to be, so they could impart their wisdom to the world without the temptation of having followers or developing their egos."

It was an interesting session, and Omaran was glad he had come home at just the right time to be a part of it. He marveled once again at the many ways they were being guided, and this event reinforced his belief that the force of the two of them together, as twin flames, was far greater than he could imagine.

Now he knew that there really were beings of darkness, and that the way to counter them was through love! He wasn't sure he could have generated a feeling of love and understanding if such a being had confronted him to do battle instead of Antera. But it seemed that the trick was to let go of all ego involvement and to recognize that everyone can be a channel of this tremendous power and force. It had been a good lesson in using the will center in a positive way, by confronting the darkness and bringing the energy up to the heart. He wondered if he could use that approach with his own demons somehow.

He went back to work, and Antera called Janet back to share the experience and guidance she'd had, and to let her know the depth of the issue. Those cosmic energies of the last few days were certainly being felt, and she wondered if all lightworkers were being similarly affected.

Twenty One

*Let the
light of forgiveness,
the light of compassion,
the light of love . . .
radiate, propagate,
and dominate
before it's too late.*

— From the song
"The Light of Forgiveness"

As they both worked at their jobs through the fall and winter, Antera and Omaran were able to slowly mend their finances. But work on the plans for the spiritual center was also very slow. It was hard for Antera to get very excited about it now anyway, because she didn't know whether she and Omaran would be together for long. She thought maybe that was one of the reasons she was back at work; maybe the center wouldn't be built after all because the twin flames couldn't even live together in peace.

Life with him was either blissful and joyful or absolutely horrible, with seemingly nothing in between. She wasn't at all sure he would be worth sticking around for, as her guides had indicated, because his progress was so slow. It almost seemed like he was getting worse, like the lows were getting lower.

After each time Omaran lost control of his anger, Antera tried to get him to seek help, anything to get him to release. She offered her own counseling services many times, but even after all these years, he still thought of her as the enemy when he lost control, and couldn't accept her help. She kept encouraging him to use the many healing tools they had been given, but he continued to resist and she was tired of reminding him. She knew that she wasn't being successful at loving him all the time. In fact, she was getting more and more resentful of him. They rarely had any pleasant conversations any more, and she sure didn't feel like making love very often.

Early the next year, starting their fifth year together, Omaran hit bottom. He was seldom present, and she decided she had had enough. She just couldn't hold up the charade any more. The dark side had won this battle, from her perspective, and she wanted to give up. It felt like she had been gradually filled up with his pain and couldn't take any more—not even a small amount. She had to do something drastic.

"I need to separate from you. I have finally reached my limit. I thought that I was able to release the pain as it came up, but now I can see that I have allowed a small amount to stick each time, and I can't hold any more pain. I need time to heal, away from you. I have had it, and I've made my decision."

They had just finished dinner, during which conversation had been strained. She had decided for sure on her commute home from work, and only waited until they had eaten to tell him.

He felt flushed, and a bit desperate. Deep within, he had never believed her the many times she had threatened to leave, because their souls absolutely needed to be together—were destined to be together. But this time she looked serious. He started to panic, and swallowed hard. "What do you mean? Where would you go?"

"For starters, I'll sleep in the living room. I simply have to be away from your energy and have time alone. I can't heal you, I just have to heal myself, and that will take time and effort. You're on your own now. I give up."

He didn't even attempt to talk her out of it; he could see that her mind was made up for now. At least she wasn't leaving the house yet. If he were good, surely she would come around again. "Is this about yesterday when I got mad? I said I was sorry, I don't mean to take it out on you. What do I have to do?"

"We can no longer be together unless you put your healing at the highest priority in your life," she said quietly, with a resolve that sent shivers up his spine. "That means every single day doing something to release your repressed energy. That means learning how to release your anger without taking it out on me just because I am here. That means loving me one hundred percent of the time, not only when you feel good, but when you feel bad as well. The love flow between us can't stop, ever. I have told you all this many times and you just don't get it. I have lost hope that you ever will."

"Well, you have to forgive me. I can't be perfect. You hold on to things too long."

She knew he was right about needing to forgive. That was what she intended to work on during her time alone. She didn't want to resent him, she wanted to love him unconditionally, and it disturbed her that she couldn't do that after all that had happened. Too much hatred had come at her, and she had been damaged. So it was time to up the ante— everything else she had tried didn't work for long. He simply had to put the effort in for healing, or lose her and all they had together. It was a lot to lose, and she hoped it would be enough to force him into action.

She said, "You take care of your healing, I'll take care of mine. While we are separated I'll talk to you only occasionally as necessary, but I'll be retiring early to have my time alone. I suggest you take this time to reassess what you are doing and why you won't get help after all this time."

"For how long?" He tried not to panic—he couldn't imagine life without her, she was his support, his teacher, his lover, his everything.

"I don't know. Depends on whether you decide to get help and heal, and whether I can still heal. But I can't live with resentment toward you, we are too close and I don't want barriers between us. I've done all I can do to help you and you simply don't want help. You continue with the same behavior. If you don't get help, we won't be together any more, period." There, she had said it. The ultimatum. Now she had to stick to it.

He went into shock, and nodded. Her mind was made up. "Um, well, you can have the bedroom. I'll sleep out here."

"Fine." She didn't argue, and had been hoping he would let her have the bedroom so she could have more privacy. She brought out the foam pad they used for guests to sleep on, and put bedding on it for him, then went into the bedroom and closed the door.

He sat down on the couch and picked up the sports page from the newspaper, holding it as if he were going to read it. But he couldn't read. *Surely she doesn't mean that she has really given up on me. I've tried, haven't I? What does she expect, perfection? If she really means that she might leave me. . . .* No, that was a possibility he could not even face. He depended on her.

He had been lost before she came along, and he had grown so much, and done an incredible amount of healing since they came together. Now they had all those plans to build the spiritual center, and teach more together . . . she couldn't be serious.

What will I do if she doesn't talk to me anymore? Or if she really moves out? Pressure was building in his throat and in his heart, a heaviness he wished he could easily relieve. He wanted to cry, but something inside always seemed to hold back the flood of tears. Though he knew how good it felt after crying, it wasn't something he could just will to happen. Why couldn't he break through and release this pain inside? Over and over again, Antera and her guides had told him that it was simply energy wanting expression—it wasn't him. He understood those words intellectually but still couldn't seem to break through whatever barrier he had. It was all just words.

Feeling miserable, he decided to think about it tomorrow, as he was too tired now to integrate all of this. He put his full attention on reading the latest about his favorite football team, then went to sleep on the mattress on the floor.

"I am forgiven, therefore I forgive. . . . I am forgiven, therefore I forgive. . . ."

Antera whispered it over and over, imagining the wave of forgiveness descending over her from her Higher Self and her guides, filling her whole being, and then radiating out to Omaran from her heart and throat. Tears streamed over her cheeks in a constant flow. She added arm movements, and it became a dance of sorrow. As she cried, she could feel her heart opening, ever so slowly, letting go of accumulated frustration and hurt from the last three years of relationship with Omaran, since his demons had appeared.

It was a process suggested by her spirit guides, and it felt very productive to be alone concentrating on her own healing process. The pain she was holding onto was far greater than she had realized before she had instigated the separation. It was a pain deep in her soul, from being apart from her twin flame for thousands of years, and desiring to be with him—and after finally finding him, discovering that he could not love her. And she had to forgive him for that, she simply HAD to! If he couldn't love her as she wanted, then she was being hurt by her own expectations of the relationship, and nothing else. Blaming him for her expectations wasn't fair, and only hurt them both.

But is expecting to be loved by my other half such a bad thing? Is it really asking too much? She wondered. *My guides did teach me to trust only in God—that if I trust in humans I will only be hurt.* Certainly, she understood that now. She had trusted in the love between twin souls, thinking that the love they had at the spirit level would be enough to break through any human barriers, but the human baggage had proven even greater than that love force. This was one of the hardest things to accept, that he didn't love her enough to overcome the demons of the past.

She worked for hours each night, first on forgiveness, then when that felt complete, on letting him go. She wanted to completely release him, to cut any energy cords between them, to release any unhealthy attachment she had to him, so only love and acceptance would remain. She called on all the masters she worked with, especially Archangel Michael with his blue-white sword of Light, to help her cut the cords. There was a lot to release. The attachments were great, but she kept at it night after night, wondering whether she would ever heal completely from him. It ripped her heart out just thinking about being apart, or seeing him with another woman. And on top of letting him go, she had to give up their plans for further spiritual work together.

Confronting the pain head-on and working through it was extremely difficult, but she knew it was the quickest, and really the only way, to completely heal and move on . . . on to a life without Omaran. She had very little hope that he would heal and live up to her demands. If he hadn't by now, he simply didn't have the desire, and/or couldn't. The relationship wasn't important enough to him. That thought brought a new wave of tears. *How can the pain he is holding onto be so much more important than our relationship? So much more important than twin flames and their spiritual connection, their spiritual service?*

It hurt . . . it hurt so much she wondered if the pain was endless, a pain of the soul that could only be healed when they did finally get back together successfully, in love, perhaps even hundreds or thousands of years from now.

Two weeks staggered by, with no changes in the relationship. Omaran was feeling lonely, missing his life companion every evening, wanting to share with her his day and hear about hers. But each night after she made dinner she put his on the table, ate hers alone in the living room, then retired to the bedroom. How long would she continue this? What was she waiting for? Her face looked strained and puffy as if she had been crying a lot. And sometimes she would come out to the kitchen to get ice, which he knew was for her eyes, to keep the swelling down. What was she doing in the bedroom? Why was she crying every night?

His loneliness became a deep sadness, and a couple of times he actually wept at the fleeting thought that she might even leave him for real. But he held that thought at bay as much as possible, hoping that she would still come around. This was getting increasingly difficult as the nights passed and nothing changed. He tried to do little things for her around the house that she would notice, so she would know he loved her and wanted her back.

He didn't feel angry now, and couldn't remember why he had been angry so much in the last few months. Was he angry at her? He couldn't think of anything about her that made him angry. She had always been loving toward him. There wasn't a mean bone in her body, she was always kind, even when she got frustrated with him for being mean to her. And she never criticized him. She had said many times that all she wanted from him was love. He did love her, so much. Far more than he had loved anyone else. The thought of losing her was unbearable. Had he lost her already? He knew she was his twin flame, and if she left, his insides would rip apart. He would never be the same again. Maybe he would not even be able to live.

Why couldn't he control his anger? Was she right that he would have to yell and beat pillows to let it out? It seemed like there was way too much anger inside for that to do much good. But he decided he was willing to do even that now, if it would really help.

After three weeks of separation had passed, Omaran was feeling the depths of loneliness, without his companion to talk to or do things with. It was Saturday afternoon. Antera was in the bedroom keeping to herself, as she often was, only coming out occasionally. He sank into despair. Fears of her leaving him for good became too much to bear. She had threatened leaving many times in the past couple of years, but he had never really believed that she would do it. But now it was happening, and the desperation hit hard. He felt completely lost. He found himself wandering around aimlessly in the back yard, not knowing which way to turn, or where to go.

He turned around, and suddenly Antera was there by the back door, watching him. He hadn't even heard her come out. He kept wandering, thinking that he could not find solace with her any more.

She asked, "Are you all right?" . . . knowing that he wasn't, for he looked like a lost little boy. She had never seen him like that, so far out of present time that he didn't even know where he was or what he was doing.

He muttered something and kept pacing.

"Would you come in please?" She gently asked.

He followed her inside. She closed the door, and put her arms around him. His whole body started shaking. She said, "Go ahead, let it out. Let it all out."

His tears started with a quivering chin, and as she held him he finally let go and sobbed with his entire body, crying out sorrow and pain that he had carried for a long time. He wailed. It felt so good to be able to let go after holding it in for so long. The sobbing continued for a long time. When it started to let up, he told her he was afraid she was leaving him for good. This brought on another wave of tears. She said nothing, letting him release. It was the first time he had ever really cried, sob after sob shaking his whole body.

In the days after, he felt like a new man, better and stronger than he had for a long time. He was still sad about the separation, which hadn't changed, but the release of pain had been so wonderful, he wished he could do more of it. He couldn't seem to find that place inside himself again that triggered the tears. He really had sunk to the bottom of the emotional pit before he could break down and let go. Would it always take such a drastic situation? It felt so good, and now he understood why Antera had been suggesting it for so long. Maybe he had cleared most of it out all at once!

Two more weeks went by, and Antera was now feeling much better. The many hours she had spent crying and delving into the pain had revealed to her just how much pain she had taken on. She was starting to feel at peace with losing the love of her life, and felt only compassion for him. She knew that if he went on to another relationship he would carry the pain of losing her as well as all the rest of the pain he already had, with him. That would poison the new relationship even more than it had theirs. But she was letting him go, and seeing him healed was not her responsibility any more. She was glad he had sobbed at last, but it was only once. She was actually starting to feel happy about the prospect of living alone for once in her life, anticipating the freedom that would give her.

"Do you want to talk?" She broke the ice after dinner one evening.

He was suddenly afraid of what she would say, and how he himself might act. "Sure, if you do."

They sat down in separate chairs. "How've you been?" she asked cautiously.

"OK." He shrugged. "But missing you. Can we at least sleep together again? I'll stay on my side of the bed, I promise. I don't want to sleep out here anymore."

She shook her head slowly. He really was missing the point. "And have you been doing any healing?"

"I've been praying for help every day, meditating on how to release my anger. I just don't know what to do. The crying I did really felt good, but I can't seem to do any more, and I know there is more pain. I know it hurts you when I attack you, I just can't seem to control it."

He seemed sincere about wanting to change, but still didn't have a clue as to how. "Do you want to get some help?"

"Like what?"

"There are lots of sources of help out there. When you really want to change, you will do the research, spend the time, and find the healing path that is right for you. Obviously the things I've suggested you haven't been able to accept, and just praying isn't working, is it?"

Her green eyes deeply penetrated his being. She was always so focused, so sharp, so right. . . . He looked down. "Will you give me some counseling sessions?" He had been thinking about asking her, and was hesitant because she always seemed like the enemy when he was mad, and that may interfere with the process. But she had volunteered many times to help him clear his energy from the past.

"Are you sure you could accept me as a counselor? I would require a commitment of three-hour sessions, three times a week, and you would have to keep appointments no matter what. I'd be happy to help only if your commitment is there, because it is a big time and energy commitment for me." She wasn't sure it would work, but if he really wanted to do it, she would give it a try. He did sound desperate.

"OK, I'll do it, if you think it will help."

She continued, "And only if you are doing it because you recognize that there are parts of you that need changing, and you really want to heal, not because I say you need it. The motivation has to come from you."

He thought about that for a few moments, nodding his head. Was he doing this for her? To keep her, so she wouldn't leave him? Partially, yes. But he knew now that he really had to heal his core issues, that if he didn't take this opportunity he would continue to have problems, if not with her, then with others.

He said, "I really do want to heal. I'm tired of being upset all the time. I want to be happy, not always reacting to others."

He meant it, she could see that. "OK, we'll start tomorrow evening. Make sure you get a good night's sleep so you will be alert, and let's see how it goes. But it doesn't mean we can be together again yet." She was very relieved at his initiative, but certainly didn't want him to know. She needed to continue to be tough. It was so hard to stay apart for long, and it took a lot of effort just to keep from hugging him, even though she had worked so hard on dis-attaching. What was it about him that she could be in love with him after all they had been through?

He was visibly relieved, and hoped she wouldn't stay away for long now. They were so connected, she couldn't fool him with that toughness. But he was willing and dedicated to getting it right this time, and could wait. Just as long as she would talk to him, and counsel him, that was a start.

The counseling sessions went well. She used counseling techniques she had learned decades ago, and which had helped her clear out old energy and patterns from her own past. They dug deep into his pain, tracing it back in time to the first cause, in this or past lifetimes. He was amazed at how so many of his attitudes and upsets came from other times, and how so many of them were connected to each other in his mind. Antera acted professional and their closeness and history never caused any problems. When they were in session, she was his counselor, not his mate, as if she took one hat off and donned another. And between sessions, they never talked about what had been revealed during them.

The long-forgotten pain Omaran addressed and released felt like a huge weight was being slowly chipped away at, and he felt noticeably lighter after each session. Sometimes even his perceptions changed as he brought more of his energy back to present time—the colors in the room looked brighter, and his hearing improved. Had he really been carrying that burden for so long?

Progress was visible and swift. He was in present time more often. His expression of love and appreciation for her became more overt. A sparkle returned to his eyes and stayed there. After a month of sessions, they were eating together again, laughing again. Antera reasoned that it couldn't be helped. And as long as he was making progress there was hope, there had to be.

His company was fun again. One evening, he sat closer to her on the couch, playfully cuddling, and before she knew it, they were making love and she couldn't keep him from their bed any longer. The attraction was too great.

"Just so you know," she said afterwards, "this doesn't mean everything is fine."

He smiled, "Oh, I would never assume that. But you'll see. I'm a new man." They both giggled and fell asleep closely entwined, nourishing each other's bodies and auras. Hugging was always the best part.

The next day she wondered if she was doing the right thing, getting back together so soon. She didn't want to lose her advantage. Since she had cleared her own energy field during those weeks of separation, she didn't feel any more resentment toward him, and when he did get upset, she was able to love him and soothe him in a way that made him come back much more quickly than he did before. And each upset was worked on in the following session. She could finally love him in the way her guides had been telling her to all along, but which had been nearly impossible before.

But even as they got along better, a voice in the back of her mind kept saying, "Don't count on it lasting, don't trust him." As long as he was working on it, she was satisfied that he would get better and better, but she could not get attached to that. At least she could love him again, and he was actually loving her as well, for a change. It felt good.

As Omaran worked through his pain, he was able to distance himself more from his anger, and finally experience what Antera and their guides had been telling him for years. He really was not his anger! He could feel it up welling in him occasionally, but instead of allowing it to take over, he recognized it as energy, simply needing expression. And the best thing was, now he could actually choose how he let it be expressed. This was major for him! He actually found that he could excuse himself if he was feeling off, and take a walk, blow forcefully, or find some other way of releasing the energy so it didn't come out at his mate. He also discovered that when he did this, the real cause of his frustration would often become apparent. In this manner, a stream of deep issues continued to arise, and were released.

Once, Omaran even brought up the old, sore subject of marriage. He casually asked her, "Do you want to get married?"

It could have been a simple question, if it didn't have all the heartbreak behind it from his earlier rejection of the idea. He was feeling like he wanted to make up for that, and seal their relationship bond, now that they were getting along so well. Now he wanted a commitment from her so she wouldn't be as quick to separate from him again. It just felt right, and he couldn't remember why he hadn't wanted to before. What had he been afraid of, anyway?

But she was wary. He would have to earn her trust back and that may take a while. She said, "Why? I think the time for that is long past. What would be the point now after we've been living together for years?"

"I just would like to. If you're not sure, I can wait, but I want to sometime."

"We'll see."

It meant a lot to her to hear him say it, more than she let on. The idea that he wanted to marry finally, after so much pain around it, started to soothe and heal that wound in her heart ever so slightly. But marry him when he could turn into a raving madman again? No, she needed to see him healed first, and that would only be proven with time.

The Council was more confident than ever that Omaran would indeed come around permanently, and continued to assure Antera that he would be worth the wait. She was starting to believe it. He was acting more like he did when they first got together, before his dark side revealed itself with such vengeance.

Their guides continued to encourage their relationship, as they always had, unceasing in their love, compassion, and support. Antera could feel an almost palpable increase of joy in the inner planes each time Omaran made a big step forward in transforming his dark energy to Light. She remembered her guidance telling her two years before, while they were camping on Mt. Shasta, that he was special, as if he had been lost for a long time, and would embody great power and love when and if he finally healed. There was no doubt that there was more joy in their lives already.

Twenty Two

I appreciate so much
that you stuck with me,
loved me, waited for me.
Now I'm asking you for trust
in my heart, in our bond,
a new start.
Will you marry me now?
I am a new man,
you'll see that I am.
Will you marry me now?

— From the song
"Will You Marry Me Now?"

I n April, they took off for the alpine town of Mt. Shasta. The couple was drawn to the mountain again and again, and it was the place they always went when they had a weekend free. It was only a five-hour drive. They generally camped in the spring, summer and fall, and stayed in motels in the winter. Every time they visited the majestic mountain, one or both of them underwent a major spiritual event, either in meditation led by their guides, or during their sleep. They were very active in the inner planes there, and it rejuvenated them. Travelling back and forth between the two mountains, Shasta and Tamalpais, they felt like human ley lines, carrying energy from one to the other.

As soon as they arrived on this trip, unfortunately, Antera collapsed in the motel room with a pounding headache and nausea, forcing her to stay in bed. In the days prior to leaving, she had just finished a project for her job that required working very long hours, to the point of exhaustion, and now she was paying for it. By Sunday she was almost recovered, and that evening they discovered their real reason for the trip.

The two of them were in their room, sitting up in bed for their nightly meditation together. Omaran got sleepy and laid down. Antera was suddenly feeling a lot of energy pouring through that felt a bit different than the masters she usually worked with, and a presence in the room slowly grew stronger.

"There is someone here, and I don't know who it is yet, but I think there will be a communication."

That was all Omaran needed to hear to sit back up, wide awake. "I don't want to miss anything," he said.

A few moments later, Saint Germain made his presence known. Antera recognized his energy, having felt it around her many times in her life, but this was their first conscious contact with him, a most magnificent being. It felt joyful to be in his company. Without wasting any time, he told them that he was there to give them an initiation as a couple. There were two other beings behind him who remained veiled, a male and a female, and after the initial blessings, Saint Germain prepared Antera and Omaran to receive a special flame, passed from the couple behind him to them. He told them that they were being given the opportunity to hold the flame in their hearts, the flame that represents the Twin Flame Archetype for the planet. This would make it easier for other twin flames to find each other and do their world service together. He warned them that if they accepted this post, there would be responsibilities that come with the energy boost.

"What kind of responsibilities?" Antera was quick to ask.

"You will be required to keep the flame stoked at all times, for eternity or until you are relieved of the job. You will have to work with it daily, to keep it alive, and make sure your thoughts are as pure as possible, because impure thoughts could extinguish it."

Antera relayed the message she heard to Omaran and they hesitated for a moment, while they considered the vastness of eternity . . . did they really want to take on such a responsibility? Could they really keep their thoughts that pure? They looked at each other, nodded, and decided to accept, knowing from past experience working with the masters that what was offered in this way was always for the highest service and never more than they could handle.

"We accept," they both said out loud.

The ceremony then continued, as the couple in the background took the flames they had been carrying for a long time and passed them into the hands of Saint Germain. He passed them to the new bearers, putting them directly into both of their hearts at the same time, and holding his hands there for what seemed to be a very long moment. Antera could feel him adjusting her energy field and opening her heart to a new level to accommodate the brilliance and purity of the flame. It was real and tangible. It warmed her heart.

The master continued talking without removing his hands. He explained that their dedication to their spiritual evolution, both together and individually, had made it possible for this honor. His speech was very eloquent, and Antera found herself thinking that she was sorry there hadn't been more warning so they could have gotten a tape recorder out and taped it. She repeated what Germain said as best she could to Omaran as he explained in more detail how to care for the flame, and that he would personally be teaching them more as time went on about how to use the flame. He answered some immediate questions of theirs, except for one.

Omaran asked, "Who are the couple who were the previous holders of the flame?"

St. Germain answered, "That will be revealed at the proper time, but for now they will remain veiled."

He ended by saying he would be back the next day, and left. Antera and Omaran were profoundly affected by the whole incident, excited but a bit apprehensive as well, not being entirely sure they could live up to the task. They stayed up to talk about it for a while, then slept very soundly.

The next day, they sat to meditate hoping that Saint Germain would again appear, and this time they had a tape recorder ready. They were greeted, instead, by the veiled couple who were the previous holders of the flame. They were still veiled, and the four of them sat facing each other, forming a diamond shape. The mystery couple telepathically invited them to create a group "Light vehicle" with them.

The foursome breathed together for a few moments to synchronize their energy fields so they would spin at the same rate, and a form was created around them, which suddenly clicked into action and they "lifted off." The resulting journey was in the inner planes, but felt very real. They could feel discernible motion, but the direction they were going wasn't obvious to the two who were along for the ride. They all quickly emerged inside a cavern with a sandy floor that was quite large, and they realized that they were inside Mt. Shasta itself! A beautiful rose quartz crystal was in the center of the group, giving off soothing heart energy and grounding them, helping them to focus their presence in the cavern. They could feel their hearts being purified and the new flames being stoked with pure Divine Essence.

Antera and Omaran were gazing at the figures and symbols on the walls of the room when Saint Germain appeared. He looked absolutely magnificent in a beautiful violet robe that sparkled, and they were both filled with awe. As they stood up to greet him, the other couple left.

"Please don't be overwhelmed by my appearance—you will appear just as magnificent when you have fully brought in your Higher Presence. This is the most important connection you can make, and I am here to aid you in making that connection even stronger, more joyous. I also wish to make sure the flame is growing, the Christ Flame in your hearts. This flame will eventually grow and completely consume every cell in the body, purifying every cell and taking them to Christ Consciousness. This is just the beginning!"

He instructed them to look up and see above them the shining presence of their Golden Self. Each watched as he helped them see it more clearly, bringing it down around them like a cloak of golden Light. "This is the part of you that does so much service in the inner planes, constantly helping others, serving God-Goddess, the One. . . . This is the part of you that *is God, is Goddess*."

Antera felt like she was growing very tall, growing into the size of her Higher Presence. She tried to stay down in the room at the same time.

"See, now you are as brilliant as me!"

She looked right into the eyes of St. Germain, and it was like looking into a universe . . . like looking all the way to Source . . . and then looking back at herself. He asked them to make a choice, right then, of inviting their I Am Presence into their lives many times a day, thinking about it often. They both were experiencing such bliss, that all they could say was "OK!"

He then led them into another room, to undergo a purification, and left the two alone. They didn't know what to expect. First, they were bathed in warm hues of Light, then Antera noticed a white Light appearing, which slowly grew brighter and brighter. The Light started to take on a human form. As features appeared, she was pleased to recognize Master Jesus standing before them, in an immense bright Light that was almost too bright to look at. He greeted them with a smile and they could tangibly feel his tremendous love. He asked them both to completely release all that was not of the Christ Light, as he continued to build up the intensity of the energy around him. He then projected the energy in their direction with such a blast that they felt it go through all their systems, stripping away any remaining sheaths with which they had clothed themselves— anything that was not aligned with the most Divine Love and Light.

"Be here with me. Be here totally in the Light, be one with us! Give up earthly vows, they mean nothing . . . give up any debts you have, they are meaningless to the Christ Light . . . give up all attachment to human nature, all attachment to ego, and step into the Light! Allow all to melt away into the Light. Become total, pure soul essence. The Christ Flame can only grow in this environment!"

It literally felt like a solar wind was blowing past them and through them. In one motion, they were purified such as they had never felt before. It was like being stripped to the core essence of their being, to the place where everything is real, where only God-Goddess can exist, exposing all else as meaningless and not needed. The Divine Love they received at that time was indescribable in words, and was felt to such a deep level that they were breathless.

As the wind died down, his farewell was, "All I ask . . . is that you love!"

He then faded and became smaller and smaller, transforming into a symbol on the wall, which looked like an eagle with spread wings. They both took a few deep breaths, and found themselves back in their motel room, as they opened their eyes and looked at each other. They hugged with tears in their eyes for the love and appreciation they felt for each other and the masters.

Over the next few weeks, Saint Germain visited a number of times, as he instructed them about how to use the flames. He also told them more about twin flame relationships:

"There have been very few twin flames that have achieved a coming together in the last of their lives on the planet. The ones who have tried, have mostly failed. In most of the pairs, one of the beings had progressed in their spiritual evolution at a faster rate than the other, and could not wait for the other to catch up. So often one had to go on, and go about their evolution, then come back as a spirit guide to the other when it was time for the other to work through their last lifetime. And that is why many twin flames are a partnership between one embodied and the other not.

"This is why what you have done is so important and unusual, coming together at this time to achieve the solidarity and the union that you now have. And even though when you embarked on your path together it may have seemed premature, it was the only way to speed up the process, the only way Higher Presence could see, to push you both into enlightenment. This chosen path of the sacred partnership is, because of all this, one that few have tread . . . you are pioneers breaking the way for others to follow."

The couple felt very blessed, and practiced with the flames. It seemed as though they had made it through, and finally had come together for real. All the major parts of them which weren't in alignment with Divine Love had come up for healing, so they could be together. What a journey! They both knew it didn't mean that they were finished with their evolution. Undoubtedly, more would be coming up as they could handle it. Evolving back to a place of pure Divine Love was proceeding quickly, but one level at a time. It was a good thing they had so much help from their spirit guides. Coming together had put them on the fast track, but certainly not the easy track! They had no regrets, but could they really recommend this path to anyone else?

Twenty Three

In the beginning,
only us, you and I.
Heaven birthed us
in a star-filled sky.
Conceived as a union,
divided in two.
Apart for lifetimes,
now that's all through.

— From the song
"Union"

A few weeks later, in late May, Omaran and Antera were sitting at dinner in a local restaurant and she found the words coming out of her mouth before she had time to think about it.

"Let's elope."

"What?"

"Let's get married."

"Are you sure you want to?"

"Yes, it seems right, finally. What do you think? How can we express the Twin Flame Archetype if we aren't even married?"

"Of course, I've wanted to for months, but I've been waiting for you to want it." He was excited. This must mean that she had finally forgiven him.

She hadn't really thought about marriage for a long time, but suddenly it seemed just the thing to do. Omaran had come a long way in his healing, and was in fact a "new man," as he had claimed. Though there were still times when he got upset easily and tried to take it out on her, those episodes were much less frequent now, and when they did occur, he caught himself before the old patterns kicked in, coming back to the present much more quickly. Their relationship had become more important to him, and he was really trying to make it work.

She said, "So when? We could just sneak off and do it, and announce it afterwards."

"Don't you want a few friends there, and our kids at least?"

"Well, maybe. The next good date would be the Summer Solstice. How about then?"

His mind quickly did the calculations. "That is only four weeks away. But it feels right." He was so glad to have the bad times behind him now. When he had really started working through his pain, it hadn't been nearly as bad as he had thought it would be—not that he thought he was done, by any means. Looking back, he didn't know why he had resisted so fervently and waited so long to get help. He thanked Spirit that Antera had stuck it out. Now they got along amazingly well, and they would actually marry, the perfect culmination for perfect mates.

They should have guessed that St. Germain was behind this idea, for sure enough he told them later that it was important to make that commitment to each other for the Twin Flame Archetype to be firmly anchored into the planet. Not that it mattered for their union, which was spiritually in place, but because it would give them more credibility in their coming service together, and it would provide some closure to their years of difficulty.

Over the course of the next few days, as they discussed it, the plan developed from eloping, to inviting a few friends, to inviting a hundred people, then back to inviting a few friends and family. The ceremony simply had to be on Mt. Shasta, there was no question, even though the location would drastically limit the number of people who could attend. They felt surprisingly joyful at planning this, as if it were the perfect thing to do, in spite of their very busy schedules.

St. Germain telepathically communicated an image to Antera over and over through the next week. She sketched it several times, trying to get it right but not sure what to do with it. It was two flames intertwining around each other, as if they were spinning. It was to be the Twin Flame logo. But would it be incorporated into the marriage ceremony, and if so, how?

She called her sister Linda, who was an artist, to see if she had any ideas. As she explained the image, Linda got excited.

"I think I know just what it looks like. I've been getting a flame image the last few weeks but didn't know what to do with it. Fax it to me so I can see it."

"Wow, that is amazing! Do you think Germain is communicating to you as well?"

"Yes, his energy has been strong. He obviously thinks this image is pretty important so there must be a good reason for transmitting it to both of us."

"Well, I guess you are elected to bring it to form, then. Any ideas about what to do with it?"

"Hmm . . . maybe I could paint it onto two medallions for you to wear during the ceremony."

"It's only three weeks away, do you think you could do that? It would be absolutely wonderful, and what a great wedding gift!" Linda was the only one in her family, besides her sons, who could make the wedding on such short notice, and Antera was really glad she would be there. They were soulmates, and very close to each other spiritually.

"We'll see. Fax it and I'll let you know."

"Thank you!" She gave a quick thanks to Germain for setting that up.

In a few days, Linda called back to confirm that the image was very similar to what she had gotten, and that she would do the paintings on wooden disks made by her good friend Ross, a sculptor who worked in wood. She and Ross felt called to travel out into the desert for a few days to perfect the design, considering this to be a sacred project, and there, in the pure energy of nature, received more information from Spirit. Exact colors and shapes were developed in their minds as they asked for the highest form these medallions would take. Upon returning to their studios, they created the magical objects.

It wasn't until a week before the wedding that Antera and Omaran first got the indication that the masters had something more planned than a simple wedding. Jesus told them:

"Perhaps you are not fully aware yet of how many beings are attracted to this event. The reason that many are attracted is that an anchoring of energy will be taking place. A beautiful entry into the Earth's strata will be created, of Divine Love and the joining of the male and female energies in a sacred way—a vortex of energies around you.

"This particular ceremony has never actually been done before. It has been attempted, but it has never been actually taken through to completion in the physical realms. If you can do this, you will be the first. And by 'this,' I mean a gathering of this magnitude of beings together, on the planet, in such a place, to bond two beings who are balanced within themselves in their male and female sides . . . who are twin flames, and have been reunited after a long time apart, and now wish to carry out the service of becoming the Archetype of the Twin Flame energies.

"The ceremony requires a purity of heart that will only come through much sitting in meditation, in preparation. If you get too caught up in the physical preparations yourselves, and forget or neglect your spiritual needs and the opening of your hearts to the next level, then the celebration and the ceremony will not be complete. . . . We even suggest that you fast for several days first in preparation, to make sure you are pure and clean in body, as well as in mind and heart. We know you want to complete this bonding ceremony in the highest planes possible, and this will only happen if you truly are open, balanced, and harmonized with each other and within yourselves. It will happen only if you are so full of the Holy Spirit that you are ecstatic, that you are blissful, that you are full to the brim!

"We very much look forward to this. You are my beloveds. I watch over you . . . always."

After this message, they quickly changed their plans to make sure they could be alone on the day before the ceremony, and planned to fast for three days before. It became even more important for all the attendees to be fully aligned with the purpose and intent of it. So they called everyone who planned to come and let them know that they would be anchoring in the twin flame energies and that each person would have a part in it.

Omaran had invited his three kids, and was concerned about the reaction they might have about the ceremony, which didn't seem unusual for the bride, groom, and their friends, but which wasn't exactly traditional, either. He knew they probably wouldn't understand the parts about twin flames and other spiritual ideas, but hoped they could accept it with grace and respect for their differing beliefs.

One of his sons couldn't attend on such short notice and his other son and daughter decided not to attend because the ceremony seemed too far out. Judgment and unresolved anger came out at Omaran when he talked to each of them on the phone. He was heartbroken. Though his pain was great, he was determined not to let it interfere with the plans or his wedding. When he sought Antera's advice, she told him to simply love them, because love heals everything. She had learned that lesson well through her experiences with Omaran's anger.

"People say things they don't really mean when they are angry," she reminded him. "It is good to keep that in mind. I had to constantly remind myself that nothing you said in anger was true, and that helped me not take your words seriously or be hurt by you more than I was."

Omaran nodded. "I remember something the *Course in Miracles* says—that you are never angry for the reason you think. I'll try to keep that in mind."

She went on, "I'm sorry they can't accept me or our way of living, but in time they probably will. It is just their own fears they are having trouble with, not us. In time, I feel like they will come around. But you can't expect them to AGREE with our beliefs, only to ACCEPT them. They have their own paths of evolution, which are different from ours."

Omaran said, "I guess in my enthusiasm I was a bit pushy with them. But no matter what mistakes have been made, it hurts now, because this moment will not happen again and they will miss it."

He felt very sad, but knew there was nothing he could do now to change their minds, and that he would have to accept their absence.

That left nine people to carry out the ceremony, including Antera's two sons, her sister Linda, Michael and Linda, and four good friends.

They had accepted that just the right people would be there, and that most of the guests would be in the "unseen" arena.

They rented a large, rustic cabin near Mt. Shasta for everyone to stay in, and on the morning of the ceremony Antera and Omaran got up early, dressed in white robes and left before most of the others got up. The ceremonial area was up a few miles up a bumpy dirt road on the mountain, accessible only by high-clearance vehicles. They had chosen it because there was a little meadow that was relatively flat, with a nice volcanic outcrop and a clear view of the peak toward the east, framed by pines. A temporary stone circle had been created, aligned with the compass directions. The day before, the two of them had spent all day there, preparing energetically.

They situated themselves off in the woods so they could be alone when the others arrived, and sat on a blanket to fill themselves with the Holy Presence. They heard the wedding group arrive, and after allowing them time to set up, they slowly walked out of the woods. The couple was already full of Divine Light, but when they felt the presence of their friends and family, plus the tremendously large numbers of unseen beings who were there, it was almost overwhelming. They were both so filled with bliss they almost couldn't move. In this heightened state of consciousness, they only hoped that the others would remember the ceremony outline.

Antera's sons played a didgeridoo duet. The deep, earthy sound helped to ground everyone. Prompted by Omaran, who took Antera's arm lightly, they walked up to a pair of Djed columns, small renditions of the ones used in ancient Egypt in ceremonies. They energetically activated them, setting up a field of energy around the area that made everything seem even more surreal. The couple entered the stone circle through the columns, which were positioned at the entrance, walked around each direction once, took off their shoes, and went into the center. The others came in pairs, taking their places around the circle. They also walked around the circle once each way, building up the energy vortex. Michael and Linda purified everyone's energy with sage and a rattle.

As they all turned to face each direction one at a time, a call was made and a blast of energy poured in. The couple then stated the reason for the ceremony and called in the beings they knew were attending. St. Germain, who was "presiding," had a small circle of stones marking his place to stand in front of the couple. As the names of many of their unseen friends were called, they seemed more fully in place: Jesus in the east, Mary in the south, Isis in the west, and Archangel Michael in the north. Metatron surrounded the whole circle. The others had specific places as well, and many others who were not named filled the surrounding area.

Omaran and Antera turned back-to-back as a friend led everyone through a beautiful visualization that built a bridge of Light between the chakras of the two of them, starting with the Earth Star beneath their bare feet to the Soul Star above their heads. The couple then turned to face each other, holding the palms of their hands together. Their hands were wrapped together with violet sashes, and each person around the circle took turns walking around the couple, sprinkling a special combination of herbs, as they gave their blessing. The sashes came off and were replaced with rings to carry the energy forward into their lives.

They stated to each other, "Let this ring be a constant reminder of our love and devotion to each other and also of our dedication to living the Twin Flame Archetype. Thank you for finding me again, and for remembering."

They turned to face the mountain and called for the blessings from the unseen beings, one at a time. They closed their eyes and embraced each master as they came forward in spirit, touching the couple on the head, the heart, or showering them with blessings. After the last of the blessings, sister Linda came forward and placed the twin flame medallions she had painted over their heads. It was their first glimpse of them, and they were gorgeous.

With that, it was time for the final act of anchoring the energy into the planet. Four people brought the Hoop of Purification into the center. This was a hoop made of wood, stones and copper that Metatron had designed and Omaran had built a few years before. As the couple hugged and the group chanted OM, the hoop was slowly lowered over them to the ground, anchoring the energy fully. It was an amazing experience to be inside that vortex!

They all became silent, then started the chant/song Omaran had written as the couple exited, formed a bridge, and the others followed under it.

Here and now, we've begun.
All of us, we are one.
From those below, to those above
We are all consumed in Love.

Epilogue

You are my twin flame,
it's almost time
to go home again.
We made a vow long ago.
Come, my love.
You are my twin flame,
time to go home again.

— From the song
"Twin Flames"

Two years later, the couple was sitting in the living room of the new passive-solar home they had designed and built themselves, right on the flanks of Mt. Shasta. It had been the very next day after their wedding when they both intuitively knew that the spiritual center they had been planning would be built on Mt. Shasta, and not in the Bay Area after all. So by the next Spring they had wrapped up their activities and taken another leap of faith, moving to their favorite mountain. Their living situation and work had almost magically fallen into place in their new town, and now they were ready to concentrate once again on their outwardly oriented spiritual work.

After the twin flame initiation they had received from St. Germain, they had been put on probation, to make sure they were really up to the task of holding the archetype. They hadn't known about this test until they were informed that they had passed, a year later. Also, the identity of the couple who had previously held the archetype had finally been revealed, in a profound experience for both of them, as they recognized in them soul family.

As they cuddled on the couch together, still one of their favorite things to do, and marveled at their blessings, Antera said, "You really were worth it after all, you know."

"I'm glad to hear it. Guess I'm the slowest learner in the world."

"Yep."

"Well, you don't have to agree," Omaran said jokingly. They both laughed. "Really, though, I'm so sorry about what I put you through. I don't know how you put up with me, I was terrible! I really appreciate it."

"You'd better!" she teased. "Anyway, now we're both better off, and it is like we were in the beginning when we first got together, before those demons reared their ugly heads."

"Yes, we are. I'm also amazed that the wonderful masters didn't give up on me. They loved me unconditionally no matter what. I was so stubborn! I really did want to hold onto all that pain! Now that I'm through most of it, I can't imagine being that way."

"Hard to fathom! In fact, I don't think I'll ever fully understand why you took so long, considering all the help you had, and all the tools you were given to work with."

Omaran had thought about this no small amount over the last couple of years. "I really think that I had a huge amount of conditioning to overcome. Way more than either of us realized. Not only the anger itself, but the programming that said, 'I don't need help. I am strong. Suck it up and take life like a man. Don't complain,' and all that. I grew up in the John Wayne period, where to express emotions was considered very unmanly."

"OK, I can see that."

"Plus the fact that in my childhood family, we never talked about important things. We never discussed problems or tried to find solutions together. I know you probably can't imagine that, coming from the family you did, where you were all encouraged to express your opinions and find solutions. We were in so much pain from our mom being sick that we learned to avoid it altogether, hiding and pretending that everything was OK, when it wasn't OK at all. That was incredibly hard for me to break through."

"So you think that is why you kept saying you were not upset when you were, and made promise after promise about doing healing work and then forgetting about them?"

"Yes, I think that is a large part of it."

"Well, my family wasn't perfect, that's for sure, but it certainly was much healthier than what you went through. I think everyone has to deal with anger at some point in their healing process. But when my rage started erupting during my second marriage, I went for help as soon as I could. I knew it wasn't normal to have so much anger, and I didn't like it. You, on the other hand, were able to live with it for many years and avoid getting help. That is what amazes me," she said.

"But see, you recognized it as abnormal, whereas I didn't. I was able to suppress it for so long that I thought I'd just be able to continue that. Even in past lives going way back, I was good at holding it in. So that was a lot to overcome."

She hugged him. "Well, I'm sure glad you finally came through. I definitely had my doubts, despite what the Council told me. Not that you're totally done yet," she warned. "So keep working on it. Deal?"

"Deal. It should help for me to review our story and go through it all again."

"Yes," she said. "Are you sure you are OK with sharing our story with the world?"

"Well, only if I can have veto power, of course. People I know may not think very highly of me if they read it. But I do think it will be useful for others who are in twin flame or soulmate relationships." He paused, thoughtfully. "I would like to hear more about what the masters have to say about it."

"OK, I'll channel tonight. I think more people than we realize will be able to relate to our experiences, and understand what we were going through. Perhaps if some people are having similar problems they won't take so long to heal. And just maybe we could dispel the myth once and for all about finding your soulmate and living happily ever after, like YOU used to think." She poked him in the ribs with her elbow.

"What, you mean even now we can't live happily ever after?" He teased back.

"I wouldn't count on it."

"Hey, that was a hard belief to give up. But I think I got it, finally. It really has been a fascinating journey since we got together, never a dull moment! And now we are getting a chance to sing together as well. We are so blessed, living here in this mountain paradise."

Beloved Mother Mary spoke to them through Antera that evening. Omaran said to her, "I'm not proud or happy about the way I acted during the last few years, and I'm trying to keep in mind that perhaps by sharing it others will be helped, especially so many men just like myself who haven't worked on their emotional bodies much. Is this true?"

Mary gently commented, "It is very natural for you to have regrets about the way you acted, and hopefully by going through it again, you can bring forgiveness to all of it, and make peace with it within yourself. There is some forgiving that needs to be done still, especially in forgiving yourself. As you re-live those moments, understanding the pain that you caused others, understanding the dark forces that came through you, you will have the energy to transform with forgiveness.

"There is always a very good reason for these things to happen. For you to take on those dark forces within you, drawing them to you and allowing expression to them, means that you were chosen to transform all of that energy into Light. And all lightworkers, if they have the strength, have been called to these kinds of tasks, to transform as much darkness as possible into the Light.

"You cannot transform darkness into Light without fully going into that darkness and experiencing it to its very depths! You must reach the bottom! You must go as deep down into the muck as you can, because then there is that much more with you, as you pull yourself out. It may be hard to understand why what you did is so important. You have transformed not only your own dark side, your own pain—you have transformed with it the pain of many, many others.

"You chose that path! Because of your great Light, because of your great spirit, you chose to take on a huge amount of pain and suffering on this planet, from others who have sunk into their dark sides. Do you not see how much easier it will be for them to pull through now that you have done it?"

It had never occurred to Omaran before that he was healing more than his own dark side. He said, "I didn't understand that part of it. I really want to complete this. I want to transform all of this energy completely."

"Bring forgiveness. You have come through most of your pain, and by reviewing it from a different perspective you'll get a second chance to really clean it up. Make sure that you have totally forgiven yourself. Be sure that you have made amends in any way you need.

"Even the greatest spirits will take on the darkness. In fact ONLY the great spirits voluntarily take on great darkness—only they CAN. If anyone else tried they would sink into it and maybe never come out! It is only those who have the pure Light of the Christ, like you two, who have come through so much already, who say, 'Yes, I am ready to take on whatever you want to give me.' And then they take it on and dig down into the mud. But when they find their way back they wash away the mud from everyone else around them, as well as themselves. It is all permanently transformed. And the Light shines brighter on the planet, because of what the two of you have done, and gone through—because of how you persevered, and finally made it through."

Omaran was touched by her words. "I can feel the Light increasing in me as you speak. I feel strength coming in. I think it would be wonderful to share that with others."

"As I hope you will. I think much good can come from it."

"Thank you, Mary."

"You are both bright Lights on the planet. You are so blessed! You are so fearless! You continue to carry on and carry on. And we truly admire that within the human sphere. We truly admire your spirited actions. I am with you always. My dearest blessings to you."

You Are My Beloved . . .
To Omaran from Antera

You are my Beloved
I knew it from the start.
From deep within, you stirred in me
the flame within my heart.

As a child I hoped and prayed
you'd join me this lifetime
but hope grew dim as time passed by,
and other men were mine.

Then when I least expected it
there you were, so bright,
I let my world be shattered and
re-form to match your Light.

Within the safety of our Love
your darkest side revolted
and tried its best to cast aside
what our souls had molded.

But darkness cannot stand against
a Light that is so pure;
doubt and fear finally fade
against a Love so sure.

'Twas worth the risk to stay with you
I've learned the Love Divine,
for you are my Beloved
and your Twin Flame matches mine.

The Story Continues . . .

T he true story of Antera and Omaran continues in their series of books *Emissaries of the Order of Melchizedek*. The first book of this series begins after they are married, in 1999, and follows their story through 2005. During that time, they are closely guided by the Ascended Masters as they move to mystical Mount Shasta, build their own house, gather experience, and carry out their highest service, especially expanding their planetary healing. Their spirit-based journey has its ups and downs as they strive to balance the physical world with the higher dimensions. With each exciting adventure, they learn powerful lessons together.

More Information . . .

For more information about products, events, webinars, the Mt Shasta Pyramid, and the Center for Soul Evolution Mystery School, join the email list and visit the websites:
www.twinsong.us
www.soulevolution.org

Facebook: facebook.com/antera.antera
Twitter: @anterashasta

Printed in the United States
By Bookmasters